Because I'm Suitable

THE JOURNEY OF A WIFE ON DUTY

ALLISON P. URIBE

CHAPLAIN AND FOUNDER OF
WIVES ON DUTY MINISTRIES

WESTBOW
PRESS
A DIVISION OF THOMAS NELSON

WestBow Press books may be ordered through booksellers or by contacting:

WestBow Press
A Division of Thomas Nelson
1663 Liberty Drive
Bloomington, IN 47403
www.westbowpress.com
1-(866) 928-1240

Because of the dynamic nature of the Internet, any web addresses or links contained in this book may have changed since publication and may no longer be valid. The views expressed in this work are solely those of the author and do not necessarily reflect the views of the publisher, and the publisher hereby disclaims any responsibility for them.

Any people depicted in stock imagery provided by Thinkstock are models, and such images are being used for illustrative purposes only.

Certain stock imagery © Thinkstock.

ISBN: 978-1-4497-4083-2 (sc)
ISBN: 978-1-4497-4084-9 (hc)
ISBN: 978-1-4497-4082-5 (e)
Library of Congress Control Number: 2012902962

Printed in the United States of America

WestBow Press rev. date: 02/17/2012

This book is dedicated to my grandma

Irene M. Castaneda

Preface

Looking at the many challenges I have faced and the challenges I continue to face as the wife of a law enforcement officer, I am so amazed at all God has done in my marriage. We face such unique marital circumstances in law enforcement, yet God's word stands true for all marriages. I know God's hand has brought me and my marriage to where it is today and I know my journey will continue.

I am honored to say I am an officer's wife, and I embrace my husband's calling. I am married to a peacekeeper and know that God is his shield of protection, because I leave my husband in God's hands. My role as a wife was not something I thought of as important in the beginning of my marriage, but now I see the calling in it. My journey will continue till I take my last breath. I know that being married to an officer was no accident; it prewritten by my maker. Being a wife on duty means many things, and perseverance is one of them.

I believe that nothing can separate what God has joined together. Everyone's marriage is precious and I hold mine dear to my heart. As written in Songs of Solomon, I found the one my soul loves, and I will not let him go. As you read my story and journey, remember that God is a God who sees everything and that because of him, we can be certain of a prosperous future.

Foreword

This book is a book like no other, because it's much more than just a book. It's a marriage/life manual, not only for today's law enforcement marriages, in particular, but also for all marriages. It is a vital resource and dynamic tool for all married couples who desire to succeed in a society that sometimes doesn't honor holy matrimony.

Allison is a very dear friend of mine. I admire her intense love for God and unrelenting passion for police officers' wives and for the well-being of officers' families. She desires for all marriages to succeed and bear much good fruit. She has an enormous passion for that and is a powerful role model for all wives, especially those of law enforcement background. God has placed her in my life as a great example of how a wife should act toward and treat her husband.

This book will aid you in establishing a God-centered and Christ-filled marriage. We all want our marriages to prosper. This book will empower you and equip you with the word of God to overcome common marriage obstacles, and with the word of God, you cannot lose! I had many struggles in my marriage as we all do, but I began to put God's principles, which are found in his word, into play in my marriage, and my marriage has gained so much ground. I believe that the result will be the same for every marriage, if you reach out and utilize this book to pave your path in this journey called marriage. This book is undoubtedly inspired by the heart of God.

It's extremely sad that a very high percentage of law enforcement marriages end in divorce, but you don't have to become part of that statistic. This is not meant to judge anyone who has gone through a divorce, because none of us can judge. God will bless everyone if we put his word and principles into action.

I speak a very special blessing to your marriage today. May it be blessed, successful, and victorious and may it bear much good and wholesome fruit in the mighty name of Jesus, our Redeemer! And what God has brought together, may no man or woman separate.

It's not by luck that marriages succeed, especially law enforcement marriages. It takes work and effort and definitely faith and trust in God Almighty!

> God bless you and yours,
> Rachel Flores,
> San Antonio, Texas police wife

CHAPTER 1

I Do

On November 23, 2001, I prepared to walk down the aisle in front of all our wedding guests and, of course, God. I remember taking the deepest breath as I grabbed my father's arm for him to escort me to the one my heart loved. As my father and I walked, I couldn't help but smile as I looked around at everyone smiling at me. Their smiles seemed to encourage me. It was encouraging in the sense that they knew we were happy, and I knew that their highest hopes would always be with us. Still, I wondered how many people in the room were mentally betting on whether or not we would last. Its sounds horrible, but it is true. How many people attend weddings and wonder about the longevity of the marriage? The walk down the aisle, for many, is the most heart-pounding, exciting anticipation a woman can ever experience. It's the moment she's dreamed about since she was a little girl, but instead of pretending while wearing a sheet, she actually is wearing a veil, and her Prince Charming is real.

Well, I finally made it into his arms. It was my husband-to-be and me . . . , and God. We stood there listening to the word of God and all the Scriptures that related to marriage. Then it was the moment we would become one. "That is why a man leaves his father and mother and is united to his wife, and they become one flesh." (Genesis 2:24). It was time to say our vows; it was time to say "I do."

We faced each other and vowed before God to love one another, honor each other, care for one another in sickness and in health, for better or worse, till death do us part. Wow! That is some heavy duty promises! But I meant it. I loved the man I was staring at in front of me. I loved the man behind him even more—the man on the cross.

Remember, I promised and vowed before the Lord. What do the words "I do" mean? In *Webster's Dictionary* the word "do" means "to bring to pass; to perform; to commit." Of course, on our wedding day, we are joyful, and it's the most exciting day of our life, but what happens down the road when something goes wrong? Do the words "I do" mean anything? The words "I do" on our wedding day then take on a completely different meaning when it comes to the trials we face in marriage. We must all ask ourselves if we can commit to these vows.

So there we were: Mr. and Mrs. Uribe. I was so excited, scared, unsure, yet certain, all in one night. This was it; I was now married, and he and I were one flesh. Of course, I didn't expect everything to be perfect, but I figured if times got tough, I could handle it. I was a new bride with lots of new roads to journey on.

When we were dating, my husband was new on the police force—he'd been on duty only for a year. He would share many experiences he had while on patrol. Once we were married I noticed he went from telling me everything to coming home and not saying much. Then it went from not saying much to not saying anything at all. I love my husband, and I wanted to know all about his day—every detail—but did he want to share that? No.

This was a completely new ball game for me. I looked back to my childhood and recalled the times my mother and father would share when he got home from work. The scene was very different. It was then I realized that our marriage was in a class of its own. When I got married, I said, "I do", to a police officer. Of course, this was not a bad thing; this was the biggest blessing of my life, although I had not realized it yet. It was when our marriage came to a crossroads that God showed me that all things are possible and that I can do all things through Christ, who strengthens me. It was then I learned that it was not my husband who needed to change but it was me.

REFLECTION

Look back to your wedding day. What were your thoughts about the vows you made?

At the time, did you say your vows to your husband alone, or did you vow to your husband and God?

What were your hopes and dreams for your marriage as you walked down the aisle?

To what do you feel God has called you in the role of an officer's wife?

Father,

As I reflect on my wedding day, I pray you will help me to understand all I vowed before you. I pray that you will reveal to me anything in my heart, in my actions, and in my speech that is displeasing to you in my role as a wife. Forgive me, Father, if I do not include you in our marriage and the struggles we face. Show me how to be the wife you have called me to be. Show me how to turn to you alone and not to other temporary satisfactions. I pray that as I reflect, the love I have for my husband will grow deeper and that I will embrace this beautiful role you called me to as his helper.

In Jesus' name,
Amen

TRUTH

_____,

(write your name above)

"For I know the plans I have for you," declares the Lord, "plans to prosper you and not to harm you, plans to give you hope and a future" (Jeremiah 29:11).

All the days ordained for me were written in your book before one of them came to be (Psalm 139:16).

In their hearts, humans plan their course, but the LORD establishes their steps (Proverbs 16:9).

Your heavenly Father

CHAPTER 2

I Now Pronounce You Husband and Wife

Five years passed, and it was about then that our marriage seemed to have an uncertain future. We went through our honeymoon phase and then went into our adjustment phase. After being a newlywed and then getting deeper into our marriage, I came to realize that my husband, my honey, actually had flaws. It all began with the usual disagreements over toothpaste squeezing, toilet paper, and kitchen cabinets, but then those differences went into new territory. Petty issues became larger, more intimate issues that left me uncertain as to the future of our marriage. There was lack of forgiveness, irritability, loneliness, misunderstandings, and lack of communication. I came to understand the term "walking on eggshells"—it is a constant echo among officers' wives. When an officer arrives home, his demeanor may vary, depending on what he encountered that day. As officers' wives, we walk on egg shells—we have to figure out how to care for or help our husbands.

I often asked myself, "Does he need to talk, or to be left alone? Does he need to rest, or does he simply need affection? I dealt with all of this alone and never thought to pray about it.

Of course, I knew in my heart that I did not want to give up. After all, we were husband and wife; we were one flesh; and I had vowed before God. I packed my bags on several occasions and attempted to leave but never made it out the door. The truth is, I didn't want to leave; I wanted to hope. Each time I packed, I yearned for a reason to fight for my marriage and stay. The divorce rate for law enforcement is 75 percent and continues to increase. I was not about to be another statistic. I wanted to be with my husband and for everything to be okay. During that time, when I contemplated on leaving him, I thought he was the one who was always wrong and he needed to change. I was a wife, but I really did not know exactly what that meant. We grow up imagining our wedding day, but no one ever tells us what happens after all the dressing up, the flowers, and the ceremony. So, I was a wife with no wisdom as to how to be the wife I'd vowed to be. This is where the beauty of God's work began in my marriage as a law enforcement wife. "He will give a crown of beauty for ashes, a joyous blessing instead of mourning, festive praise instead of despair" (Isaiah 61:3).

I am blessed to be able to stay home and care for our children. My days are full of laundry, dishes, cooking, and lots of cleaning up. It was during an afternoon of vacuuming in my living room when I decided, once and for all, to talk to God. I knew of God all my life, but I never had a relationship with him. God was someone I went to visit on holidays at our local church. But, during such a difficult time in my marriage, I knew God was a higher power, and I knew if I prayed, he would hear. I shut off my vacuum, looked up, and said, "God, there has be more than just this. What do you want me to do? My husband needs to change. I don't get him. I don't understand. I feel lonely. Please help me. Please save my marriage. Save me." That was the best conversation I had in all my life with God. It was at that moment that God transformed my life. It wasn't my husband who needed to change; it was me. I decided to focus on God and not on my circumstances.

"Therefore, if anyone is in Christ, the old has gone, the new has come"(2 Corinthians 5:17). I decided to attend church that weekend and gave my life to Christ. I went to the altar and passed off my marriage, my children, and my home, as these were better off in God's hands. It was his to take from the very beginning. "Cast your cares on the Lord and he will sustain you"(Psalm 55:22). We are brought up to marry in a church and be married in the eyes of God. Rarely, are we brought up to remember that our marriage is God's in the first place. Marriage was God's idea, his plan for men and women. A wife of an officer once told me, "I invited God to my wedding, but I never invited him into my marriage." Marriage is supposed to be the example of Christ's love for the church. If we leave our marriage in God's hands, he will give us beauty for ashes, he will sustain our marriage, and he will bless it. With God's help, you can model your marriage according to his will.

REFLECTION

Does your marriage display Christ's love?

Do you feel there are distractions in your life that keep you from seeking God's will in your marriage (For example, pride, selfishness, greed, laziness, fear)?

Is God truly at the center of your marriage? Have you given your marriage to God?

What steps will you take to ensure God is or stays in your marriage?

Father,

I praise you for the gift of marriage and the man you have placed in my life. Forgive me if I take my marriage for granted or have lost sight of what it means to make promises to another. Help me as a wife to carry out my vows and all I promised to my husband on our wedding day. Reveal to me anything that may be distracting me from becoming greater in you and great as a wife. Help me to ensure that my marriage remains with you. I ask that you take this marriage of mine and as you did in the wedding at Canna, turn it into wine. Make it rich, sweet, blessed, and abounding with your grace.

In Jesus' name,
Amen

TRUTH

_____,
(write your name above)

"Therefore, if anyone is in Christ, the old has gone, the new has come" (2 Corinthians 5:17).

"Cast your cares on the Lord and he will sustain you" (Psalm 55:22).

"He will give a crown of beauty for ashes, a joyous blessing instead of mourning, festive praise instead of despair" (Isaiah 61:3).

"We live by faith, not by sight" (2 Corinthians 5:7).

Your heavenly Father

CHAPTER 3

How Do I Love Thee

God officially had my marriage in his hands. I had to let go and let God. Being new to Christ and new to church, I found myself excited and touched so deeply in my spirit that I wanted to live for my God. I wanted to be everything God wanted me to be. "For I know the plans I have for you, declares the Lord, plans to prosper you and not harm you, plans to give you a hope and a future"(Jeremiah 29:11). God's plans for our marriage, my life, and the lives of my children would be so amazing, our minds never could have conceived it. I shared with my husband the great things—the truth I was being taught at church. I was on fire for the Lord. It was then that this new creature in Christ vowed to be the best wife and mother I could ever be. I promised my husband and I promised God that I would fight for my marriage. I had no idea what I was really saying. What was I going to have to do in order to stay focused on my goal to save my marriage? All the fighting I did was on my knees in prayer. I realized I was suitable and that God had placed my husband in my life because I was a suitable helper for him. No one else could fulfill that task of being his wife other than me. Love was what I discovered during that time. It was the love of God that filled me with joy, and it was the love for my husband that kept me focused on the one who can makes all things new. Love would definitely conquer all. But what does love really mean?

I opened my Bible and read the Scripture definition of it. I thought to myself, *"Allison, you have a lot of work to do."* This is where all the new and exciting things came in my marriage. The definition of love is found in Corinthians 13:4-7. Living out the Corinthians description of love is something God teaches us in time and something in which God has continued to guide me. Corinthians 13 has blessed my marriage beyond expectation, and my journey through it was full of joy, correction, and patience, and followed by blessing.

"Love is patient, love is kind. It does not envy, it does not boast, it is not proud. It does not dishonor others, it is not self-seeking, it is not easily angered, it keeps no record of wrongs. Love does not delight in evil but rejoices with the truth. It always protects, always trusts, always hopes, always perseveres" (1 Corinthians 13:4-7).

After reading that, I immediately knew the love I was expressing toward my spouse was not even close to such a description. I decided to dissect the verse and seek God's wisdom on how the love I showed my spouse would reflect God's definition of love. Of course, my love may never line up to such a degree, but with God, I wanted to strive to come as close as possible. Learning to love as Christ did is one of the most amazing feelings one can experience. Who better to love in such a way than our spouse? Going deeper in our walk with God and seeing through the eyes of God can bring one to tears. Love brings about expression and the desire to fulfill an unselfish task. The most beautiful expression of love recorded in history is that of the cross. It is the image of our Savior stretching out his arms and dying for each and every one of us. The beauty of his unselfish love and his dying for our sins so that we may have life—such beauty cannot be compared. No one can understand such love or comprehend its power.

God's word says in Genesis 2:24, "This is why a man shall leave his mother and father and be united with his wife and they shall become one flesh." If we are one flesh, hurting my spouse would be hurting me. It's so true because when one of us hurts, the other hurts. If we argue, both of us are upset. If we are happy we both rejoice. We are one. What I do to my husband, I do to Christ. I love God and want to seek to express my love in an unconditional way. That brought me to the question of how much I loved my husband. How much was I willing to sacrifice? Let me count the ways. My pursuit to love him in such a way became my mission. I wanted my husband to know that I would always be hopeful; I would always protect our marriage; and my love for him would persevere.

"I found the one my heart loves, I held him and would not let him go" (Song of Solomon 3:4). We marry our spouses because of the love we have for them, and we believe it will be until death do us part. My husband is the love of my life. He is a gift from God, and I have every intention of doing my best to take care of him. At times, it may seem unfair to give so much love without knowing if I will receive it in return. It's then that I look at the cross and see such love being expressed without any expectations. It is a choice we must all make when it comes to our ways of expression and how we live out our lives. It is a surrender in which we say that all the things we do in life will be for the glory of God. Once we take our focus off our circumstances or off our spouse, we can begin to focus more on God and soon see the light. We also can begin to see God's promises fulfilled. Love will bring us to action, and our faith will be put into action.

REFLECTION

Is the love you express toward your spouse Christ-like?

Read Corinthians 13:4-7. What does it mean to you?

Reflect on the cross and its meaning. Do you feel you fully understand the sacrifice made for you to have eternal life and the love expressed from God?

What steps will you take to ensure the love you show toward your spouse will reflect the description of love in Corinthians?

Father,

I praise you for the unconditional love you have for me. I may never fully comprehend the greatness of your love, but I want to. I ask that you would help me see my spouse through your eyes and help me show him the kind of love that is expressed in Corinthians. I pray my words, actions, and love will reflect you and that my life will be a testimony of grace and love. Help me to be salt and light in the earth. I pray that as I seek to understand such love that you would protect my heart and mind from any distractions. I will search for you, my God, and I know I will find you and bring you into my marriage each day.

In Jesus' name,
Amen

TRUTH

_____,
(write your name above)

May the God of hope fill you with all joy and peace as you trust in him, so that you may overflow with hope by the power of the Holy Spirit (Romans 15:13).

You make known to me the path of life; you will fill me with joy in your presence, with eternal pleasures at your right hand (Psalm 16:11).

Blessed are those who hunger and thirst for righteousness, for they will be filled (Matthew 5:6).

And this is the testimony: God has given us eternal life, and this life is in his Son (1 John 5:11).

Your heavenly Father

CHAPTER 4

Love Is Patient, Love Is Kind

As I began this new journey with Christ and began to embrace my role as an officer's wife, there were many obstacles and days that just weighed me down. Many doubts and fears came to my mind. It was a battle-field. Patience was something I had to learn to have and am still learning to this day. I had to learn to have patience with the Lord and learn to have patience with my spouse. I had been praying for my marriage to be saved and that God would change my heart and remove anything that was displeasing. Why was patience so hard? I prayed daily and of course, many challenges came my way where my patience was tested. I realized that even though I gave my marriage to Christ, I had to put my faith into action and my actions had to be in faith!

We serve a mighty God who is the same today, yesterday, and forever. Our God sees ahead and has a purpose and plan for our life. So now that I had given him my marriage, I had to wait upon the Lord and trust in him to move in my marriage. One of many things I learned is that delay is not denial when it comes to God's plan for us. I had to have patience in my everyday life. As I began to seek God and have the desire in my heart to change as a follower of Christ, I noticed that my responses toward my spouse were not always so sweet. For example, I would get irritated at the thought of his taking a nap. When he would sit in front of the television, I would have an internal fit, or I would snap at him when he asked a question at times. It was not that he was doing anything wrong, but it was that I was not satisfied with the fact that things were not going my way. My decision to follow Christ would mean a dying of my selfish flesh. It took time and patience for me to grow and to become the helper God wanted me to be. It took time for God to help me be more patient. After all, it was not me who became patient; it was God in me and his help that gave me the ability to have such patience and grace.

My responses toward my husband began to change as God molded me. Although my day was filled with dishes, laundry, vacuuming, cooking, cleaning, and caring for our children, my husband's day was very different. His day was filled with yelling, battered women, dead bodies, abused children, murders, molestation, and much more horrific circumstances. Compare the two. I am not saying that we, as wives, cannot feel discouraged or exhausted from our daily duties, whether in the home or the work place, but officer's duties carry much stress. They have to cope with the dark valley's they walk each day. An officer can come home and take off his uniform, but inside, he is still a cop. Inside, he is fighting all he faced and is doing his best to transition to his role of husband and father. Our husbands walk many dark valleys on the beat, and we expect them to transition to these roles as if what they dealt with was of no importance or as if it never happened. Many would prefer not to be asked about their line of work, or they might even limit sharing about all they encounter. Officers witness what others would do their best to avoid. So when someone asks them about work, whether it's their wife, friend, neighbor, or stranger, most of the time they will downsize the many challenges they face. It

Chaplain Allison P. Uribe

is easier to view it as something of no importance than to view it as important and have to face such darkness head on. This can cause much added stress. It was God who reminded me that dishes in the sink are a blessing because that meant my family had food to eat. The pile of never-ending laundry also was such a blessing, because it meant my family had clothes to wear. The children and their messes were even more of a blessing, because that meant they were healthy enough to run, laugh, speak, and so much more. You see, we are blessed beyond measure. We can view these blessings either as a burden, which the enemy would love, or as a blessing. We must seek God's help in having patience as an officer's wife. Because of the stress our husbands' face daily, a patient spirit is a must. Showing them patience is showing them love.

Having learned that, I began to view my husband's daily naps after work as a way of expressing my love to him. Although I could never understand what he saw or faced, I could understand that he was on a battlefield and the only place he now felt safe, was at home. Our husbands are like soldiers fighting a war and when they come home, their war wounds are hidden in their hearts and minds. So, now, a nap was something I encouraged. It was my way of saying, "Honey, rest." I felt comforted, knowing my husband made it home safe, and now he could be in his heavenly substation—his home. I grew to seek selfless decisions more and more. By changing my ways and seeking to be more like Christ, my marriage was beginning to feel blessed and full. I was finally experiencing joy, and my patience for my husband was growing. Patience brought a peace to my spirit. God helped me through many situations when it came to my patience, and all I had to do was ask. It took time to be more understanding, but I had to remember that because I love God and because I love my husband, I was going to be sure that I was more patient when it came to growing in Christ and being the helper God called me to be.

Once I had a better understanding of how to be more patient, it helped me to be more kind.

We get so caught up in life and daily activities that we can lose sight of showing kindness, whether to others or to our very own family. Love is kind! Now that I was getting into the groove of things, as God was revealing so much to me, I wanted to be more loving, patient, and kind. I would clean the house and carry on with my daily routine, but I never really went out of my way to do extra things for my husband. It was then I decided to leave little love notes in his uniform pocket or his wallet. There were also times when I would shine his boots for him or prepare his uniform for the next day by laying it all out for him. I would remember his favorite dishes and cook them more frequently. As for the naps, I would get the bed ready for him and then do a quiet activity with our kids so his nap would be a peaceful one. Kindness took on a whole new level in our household.

"Truly I tell you, whatever you did for one of the least of these brothers and sisters of mine, you did for me" (Matthew 25:40). This should speak to us in the sense that whatever we do unto our husbands, we do to God. So how can we not be kind, loving, and patient? This verse should be a reminder to us that by going the extra mile to care for and love our spouse, we are honoring God. We honor God when we do as he has asked us to.

Now that I was doing many random acts of kindness toward my spouse, do you think I expected him to do the same in return? You bet I did! The flesh is weak. I loved how it felt to treat my husband with such kindness, but there was a little voice in the back of my mind saying, "You do all these things for him, but what has he done for you?" It was another back and-forth battle in my mind. It was also a battle of the heart, and those thoughts came from there. I remembered that I was doing it for the Lord and tried to live unselfishly—love is not envious. I found myself getting back to my old mentality and wondering why I had to do everything and sacrifice my time when I was getting nothing in return. I asked God to help me understand and realize how blessed I was. I saw the cup as half empty for a while. I battled this matter for some time, and then one day, while sitting at a stop light, my husband placed his hand on top of mine, looked me in the eyes, thanked me for being such a great wife, and said I made him happy. That was the most rewarding and special moment and I will never forget it. Why? Because I knew then that my husband had noticed! He'd noticed the random acts of kindness. That moment was better than any physical gift I could have received. It felt good to me, because I knew my husband felt loved. That was like God rewarding me for putting my faith into action.

We serve a God who sees everything. He sees you! He sees the sacrifices you make each day, the tears you shed, the long nights with a crying baby, the worry you face when you see a newscast with an officer-involved shooting. God delights in those who seek his will and love his children. "Blessed are the peacekeepers for they shall be called the sons of God"(Matthew5:17). When I read that verse, I think how amazing it is to be married to someone with such a calling in his life. I am married to son of God. Knowing that, I knew that not only would I have to be patient, kind, and not envious, but I would not to be boastful.

Being boastful and self-seeking in a marriage can be so easy. Have you ever reminded your spouse how you always clean the house, get up early with the kids, help pay the bills, that you have to do everything? Why is it that our flesh wants recognition? Love is not boastful. A boastful spirit is such a selfish spirit. It hurts me to think of how many times I reminded my husband about how hard I worked around the house and no one noticed or appreciated it. It also hurts so much to think that my husband, as a police officer, goes out each day and literally puts his life on the line to serve and protect our city, without ever receiving recognition. How many people go up to a police officer just to say, "thank you?"

I was reminded of Colossians 3:23—"Whatever you do, work at it with all your heart, as working for the Lord, not for human masters, since you know you will receive an inheritance from the Lord as a reward. It is the Lord Christ you are serving." This verse set me free from a spirit of boastfulness. In everything I do and say I want it to glorify God. Psalm 24:1 it says, "The earth is the Lord's and everything in it, the world and all who live in it." All the blessings in our life are the Lord's. This includes our family, home, children, and job. These are all blessings that were given to us to care for. For example, if you were given a gift from God, wrapped in a beautiful box, would you throw it away? Mistreat it? Put it on a shelf to gather dust? Of course not! Sadly, if this was a gift given from a co-worker or friend we might "re-gift" it, or exchange it, or even toss it out, but it is so different when it is from God. It is so important to remember how blessed we are and that because everything belongs to the Lord, we must work and care for these blessings as if we are doing it for the Lord. We can choose to see everything as a blessing, or we can choose to see everything as an inconvenience.

I was at a point in my life when I wanted to make my God smile and make my heavenly Father proud. It was glorifying him and not Allison Uribe. This obedience brought so many blessings. How can we receive more blessings if we can't care for the blessings we possess now?

There are many ways to care for our blessings gracefully and in a way that is pleasing to the Lord, including in our speech. We use words every day! We speak them, we hear them, we write them, and now, we text them. Words are defined as speech, talk, a way to express one's emotions, or promises. Words, no matter how you use them, can leave an everlasting mark or an unforgettable impression on the one who hears them. Have you ever said something you regret? I am sure we all have at one time or another. "Do not let any unwholesome talk come out of your mouths, but only what is helpful for building others up according to their needs, that it may benefit those who listen" Ephesians 4:29. Imagine if you walked around with a sign on your back but you had no clue what was written on that sign. Would that make you uncomfortable? Whether you realize it or not, when you speak poorly about another, it is like that person walking around with an invisible sign or label on his or her back. It leaves an impression to the others who have heard it. This brings me to "love does not dishonor."

We hear criticism and gossip far too often, everywhere we go. You can hear it at the store, parties, on social networks, in the news, entertainment shows, magazines, and sadly in churches. Why is this prevalent? Why is it so easy to insult another and to build ourselves up to mask our faults and weaknesses? As a wife, I find that my speech can be a weapon, and I can choose life or death in what I speak about my spouse or our children. Proverbs 18:21says, "Death and life are in the power of the tongue, and they that love it should eat the fruit thereof." Our husbands' occupation requires that they carry an armed weapon or Taser. They receive special training to handle these weapons. We trust that all officers have knowledge of how to handle these weapons and use them in wisdom. Have you ever thought about your mouth as a weapon and that the words that come out of it are like bullets? When we shoot out words, we decide whether it will be of life or death. For example, when my kids have misbehaved I tell them they have made a bad decision rather than telling them they are bad. I would prefer to build my kids up and not tear them down. Now that we know the power of the tongue, how can we change our words to bring life into our home and into our marriage?

We can speak words out of love, thoughtfulness, anger, bitterness, or insult. It can be easy to criticize our spouse when times get tough. The way we express ourselves should be healthy and godly. Ephesians 4:26 says, "Be angry and sin not." When we get the urge to open our mouths and just vent or complain, why not vent and complain to God? He knows our hearts and sees the depth of our soul, yet he still loves us. God is the only one who can help us and guide us into a victorious life.

I recall a time when I got irritated with my husband about a few things. It was getting late and I was being quite silent as to ensure not to use unpleasant words. My husband went to sleep, but I was so agitated that I decided to write him a letter, explaining my frustrations and anxieties. Once I completed that letter, my flesh was totally satisfied. I left the letter on the counter, knowing he would see it in the morning before he went to work. As I lay down, I started praying about the situation. I felt convicted and could not sleep. I could hear God saying, "Allison, why couldn't you have just told me all that? You know that I hear your cries and will give you a spirit of joy, and peace, and sound mind. I am the only one who can promise you joy in the morning." That hit me so hard that I got up out of bed, went into my closet, and read the letter to God while I cried. My husband never knew about the letter. Who was I to lay an extra burden on him? We were never intended to carry the burdens of the world or the burdens of others. In our husbands' line of work, we have no guarantee they will make it home. Of course, no one has a guarantee in life, but with the work they do to serve and protect, the chances increase.

Once I read the letter to God and prayed, I trashed the letter and was grateful that the Holy Spirit convicted me. I would have been devastated if my comments in that letter were my last words to my husband. It was full of criticism, anger, resentment, and nagging. Our words have the power to damage or build up. We must build up our spouses, children, and our home with the words we use toward them. If you find yourself unable to control your tongue, prayer is the best solution. Even God says to pray for our enemies. I'm not saying that your husband is your enemy, but in times of anger, it is best to leave it all in the hands of God. We should strive to have a Christ-like mentality and to notice the goodness in others. Once we have a greater outlook, we will see the amazing potential God has for each one of us. We will see others as God's workmanship and treat them with extra grace. We should never dishonor another with our words. Put your faith into action. Put your faith in God to handle such situations and act on it by remaining in joy, patience, understanding, and grace.

Although prayer is the solution to many situations, requesting prayer can take on a whole new level. We can dishonor our spouse or others in the way we present a prayer request. This is something that happens way too often. For example, an individual asked me to pray for a couple. When she asked me to pray, she gave me details that were irrelevant.

The situation involved a sick family member, but she offered the details about other aspects in their marriage and all they went through. Was that necessary? No. God knows the needs of each person. When asking another to pray, ask yourself what information is absolutely necessary, especially for your husband or marriage. Many times, prayer requests can be used to mask our flesh's desire to gossip or belittle another. When seeking prayer for your marriage or your spouse, be sure to use caution with whom you share your valuable information. Also, when you ask for prayer over your spouse make sure your request honors him and protects him. I recall a time when my husband upset me. I thought it best to seek prayer and when I asked someone to pray for him, I told that person about what he did and that he always upsets me. I even mentioned other times prior to that and found myself criticizing him. All of that was unnecessary. There was no reason to include my frustrations into what is one of the greatest gifts from God—prayer.

Prayer is such a powerful blessing. It is our one-on-one communication to God. When we pray, we can pray out blessings, and we can praise God for all his goodness and mercy. We take time to ask God to forgive us of our trespasses, and we know that God is so good to us that he keeps no record of our wrongdoings—his grace is that sufficient! When we pray for our spouse, the words we use should be of blessing. Let us speak the word of truth over our husbands. It is God's word that transforms. When speaking and believing for blessings in our lives and in the lives of our spouse, there is nothing more discouraging than to be reminded of our past faults. Love keeps no record of wrongdoings. When arguing, couples often remind each other of past mistakes in order to hurt their spouse. Doing such things brings about resentment and breaks the spirit.

"Forbearing one another and forgiving one another, if any man should have a quarrel against any: even as Christ forgave you, so also do ye" (Colossians 3:13). We should set an example and be a living example of forgiveness and grace toward our spouse. Knowing you are not forgiven is something that is too much for any person to bear. It is unnecessary weight for one to carry. Let's observe the Sam Brown belt—the duty belt your spouse wears while on duty. The Sam Brown usually holds the gun, handcuffs, flashlight, bullets, and keys. Have you ever tried to carry it or even hold it for a while? It is very heavy. And our lack of forgiveness is just extra load for our husbands to carry in the spiritual. Lack of forgiveness is like a gun that shoots to harm, cuffs their ability to move forward, and shines more light on their faults. It is like a lodged bullet in their heart, and is like a room they can never get out of, because the forgiveness they seek is the key to helping them feel free. Ask God to help you forgive your spouse when you find it hard to do so. If there is anger or resentment in your heart, seek God's peace and wisdom to help remove you from such bondage. When any quarrel arises, ask God to be a part of it, so it may end in peace. Your spirit will be forgiving, and your mind will keep no record of wrongdoings.

When we choose to pray and leave the burdens of our marriage in God's hands, we are protecting our marriage. Love protects! We must protect our marriages. Many of the issues we face in our marriages go back to whether we will expose our spouse or protect him. Let me give you a classic example. This example is something that usually happens at the beginning of a marriage, and at times it may be a good thing, but most of the time it can be damaging. Have you ever had an argument with your spouse and wanted to be comforted, and you immediately called your mother? I have been guilty of this. I remember when we first got married, we disagreed so much that I feared our marriage would not last. I would call my mother in tears and tell her all about our disagreements. Most times, she would defend my husband, but other times, she would get upset at the situation. I remember her telling me once that he was a good man, and she knew he would be a great husband. She remembered all I had told her about him when we were dating. Remember when you were dating, and you told your mother how sweet, attentive, exciting, responsible, understanding, and brilliant he was? Then you got married, got into an argument, and all of a sudden, he wasn't understanding; he was now boring, inattentive, irresponsible, cold, and lazy. What happened? If you are a mother, you will understand that the protective motherly instincts will kick in. All of a sudden, this blessing of a son-in-law turns into the enemy in your mother's eyes. This will make family gatherings uncomfortable, because even after you forgive him, your mom still has in her mind those tears she saw on your face or heard in your voice. Protect your marriage! Everything your marriage faces does not have to be shared with family, friends, or through social networks. Once you share too much information about your spouse or marriage, you allow others' opinions to enter your life or situation. Those opinions or thoughts may not always be encouraging or bring life to your marriage. When faced with marital challenges, protection should be your top priority. Would you allow someone to go into your bedroom unannounced, or to take pictures without your knowing it? Sharing your private details is like allowing another person into your most private area and allowing them to see more of you than is needed. Your husband should be able to trust you.

"The heart of her husband safely trusts in her" (Proverbs 31:11). In a marriage, both partners should always feel trusted and know they are safe with each other. One way to be a trustworthy spouse is for your spouse to know that God is at the center of any decision, action, or word you do or say. This all goes back to speaking life into your marriage and being an example of Christ's love.

I recall a time when my husband shared a weakness of his with me. I was very moved that he trusted me enough to know I would not be quick to anger but instead would be quick to pray. When your husband feels he can trust you, he will then feel safe enough to go to you for anything. It is something you must show him he can do. If he messes up or does something to upset you, how do you react? Do your actions show him you can be trusted with bigger things? A man does not want to be nagged at or yelled at; he simply wants to voice his concern and seek to fix it. When my husband shared his weakness, I listened, prayed to myself, and let him know that I was there for support and to be a prayer partner for him. When it comes to our weaknesses, it is not about another person but about ourselves. When our spouse shares something, it is not to be taken personally but to be taken with grace. Receiving your husband with grace allows him to feel safe and know he can trust you. As wives, we want to feel safe in the arms of our loved one. As women, we want to be heard and know that all we share is safe and protected. Trust goes beyond words and involve many situations a marriage may face, such as finances or infidelity. When we leave our weaknesses and transgressions with God, he is very gentle with us and is graceful. He is not a condemning God who points his finger in our face and grows angry. We must keep in mind that we mess up on a daily basis, and sometimes we make the same wrong decisions continuously. God is patient and continues to walk with us and teach us each time when we seek his forgiveness. As wives, we must remember to see our spouses through God's eyes and do our best to show the same grace to them that God has shown us. It is written that we should forgive as Christ has forgiven us. Such grace expressed to your spouse will lead him to have a trust in you that no one can take away. Trust is something God can help you with and something God can show you to have where needed. In leaving our trust issues with God we express hope.

Hope is defined as "to expect with confidence." Hope is something that we express when we pray. When we pray, we are saying we trust God to handle our troubles, and we have a hope that all is well. Hope in a marriage is important, because love hopes!

There were many days in my marriage, as I was seeking to fulfill my mission, when I lost hope. There were moments and days when I saw no change, and no matter how hard I tried, my situation seemed at a stand-still. It was at times like those that I knew I had to focus on the word of God and realize that by believing in the word, there would be hope for our marriage. God is always working behind the scenes in our favor. We must always remember that delay is not denial; it is simply God's way of working out the best possible plan and path for us. I'm reminded of the story of David and Goliath. I knew I had the word of God to stand on against all I faced. All the things I was going through and all my frustrations were like a huge giant that I felt I could not defeat. Although I felt like I stood alone, I was never alone or forsaken. God never forsakes us. I knew each day that I would get up and face new challenges or the same ones, and it was up to me to face them head on or walk away

Chaplain Allison P. Uribe

and lose hope. I took each day as a time to grab the word of God and speak it into my marriage. The word of God was my stone against the giants of the day. We all have David and Goliath moments. We all face challenges and situations that may seem like giants to us at the time, but once we realize how powerful the word of God is, we will see that it is the word that knocks down and moves those giants we face.

As wives of law enforcement officers, one of the biggest giants we face is divorce—it is everywhere, but there is a higher likelihood of divorce in this line of work. Be hopeful—hope in a God that makes all things new and moves mountains, which makes him mighty to save all things, including our marriages. Our marriages should be based on hope for a prosperous future. When we have such strong hope, the love in our marriage will persevere.

The battle is on for our marriages today. The fight can be so exhausting at times that divorce seems like the only way. To say there is no hope is to limit God's power. Our God is a God of hope, and with him, we can persevere. I had to train my mind to focus on the truth and on things of hope, so that I could remain focused on my goal to save my marriage. Love perseveres through all! When we act in love, we grow stronger. With all the battles we face as wives, we must decide if we are going to allow them or if we are going to do something about them. I am not talking about revenge against our spouse; I'm talking about revenge against divorce. It is looking at divorce head on and choosing to stand against it. Being a wife on duty requires a watchful eye of the things that go on in your household. It is also being equipped with the word and armor of God, so that if any harm enters your home, you can stand against it. We must fight to take back our homes.

In the beginning years of my marriage, I packed my bags several times but never made it out the door. I packed while angry, frustrated, fed-up, hurt, and feeling uncertain. Drastic decisions should not be based on our feelings but on wisdom. Each time I packed, I did it with hesitance and fear. After all was packed and the closet and drawers were empty, I stood there alone, and then I began to think things through. Why couldn't I have done that to begin with? I asked myself if I was ready to give up, if all my frustrations were valid, if I loved him enough to stay, and if this was best for the lives of my children and our future. I praise God now that even though I might not have turned to him then, he spared me that devastation. The last time I packed, I knew that was the last time and I would never do it again. I felt as if it was unfair torture and a threat toward my spouse. Even in my greatest hurts and frustrations, no one deserves that, because we all fall short. The last time I packed, I then put all my possessions back in their rightful spots. I decided I was going to do all it took to persevere in what I vowed to do at the altar.

I was watching an old television program called *The Wonder Years*. In this particular episode, the wife sat at the kitchen table, preparing dinner and listening to her children talk. Her husband pulled up, and she heard a loud slam of the car door. She knew her husband had had a bad day and immediately warned the children that their dad was upset, and they should be mindful and keep peace in the home. I watched her as she went about her day in the rest of the episode, and I noticed that she remained calm and was quick to be a helper to her husband. She went about her day with grace, and although his attitude was awful, she remained reverent, as did the children. As the episode went on, her husband's attitude went from anger to calmness. Now, if this was an ongoing scenario, maybe divorce would be looked at, but by her actions, her household regained its peace. *The Wonder Years* took place in the 70's, when divorce was not an option or an entertained idea. I observed that the wife in this show knew what it was to persevere. We must remember that we battle not flesh but against principalities in the heavenlies. We are not battling our spouse but things in the heavenly realms. Knowing this, how can we not fight and persevere in our marriage?

REFLECTION

Read Corinthians 13:4-7 and write it down. Pray, and ask God to help you love in such a way. Ask God what he is revealing to you through this verse.

Do you see yourself as a person of patience? Recall times in your marriage where your patience was tested. What will you do to ensure those future events will be handled with patience?

Random acts of kindness are usually geared toward people we don't know or in the work-place. Practice random acts of kindness toward your spouse. Write down some ideas.

If you were to ask your husband if his heart trusts in you, what do you think he would say?

Do you feel you protect your marriage? If yes, what do you do to protect it? If not, what will you do to protect it?

Chaplain Allison P. Uribe

Is there lack of forgiveness in your heart? This is something you need to pray about and wait to see upon what God reveals to you.

Does the description of your husband in your mind and to others build him up or tear him down?

Do you surround yourself with others who speak in blessing or cursing? Is your speech affected by the company with which you surround yourself?

In times of trouble, who is the first one you turn to? Is it a friend, family member, or co-worker? Why this person of choice?

With all the people in this world to seek comfort from or talk to, how can you make seeking God your top priority when you face any difficulty?

What does perseverance mean to you? What does it mean to your marriage?

Father,

I praise you for the love you expressed on the cross. Your sacrifice redeems me and makes all things possible. I pray that my love shows patience and brings about kindness. I pray that in all I say and do, you will be glorified. I pray that my spouse and my children will see the love of Christ through me. I ask that you would reveal to me lack of forgiveness in my heart. Help me to forgive as you have forgiven me. Help me to forgive in such a way that I would never keep a record of my husband's wrongdoings. I pray that I would see others through your eyes and be salt and light in the earth. I ask that you protect my mind and my thoughts from things unpleasant and unholy. Please surround me with those who know your truth and your word so that I will be around those who will speak blessings and life to me. Help me to fight for my marriage on my knees and persevere in my journey as a wife on duty. Thank you, Lord, for being in my life and for being the best friend to whom I can turn in anything I face. I praise you for the expression of unconditional love you have for me. You are a faithful God and deserve my praise. I will seek you all the days of my life.

In Jesus' name,
Amen.

TRUTH

_____,
(write your name above)

And so we know and rely on the love God has for us. God is love. Whoever lives in love lives in God, and God in them (1 John 4:16).

How good and pleasant it is when God's people live together in unity! (Psalm 133:1)

If it is possible, as far as it depends on you, live at peace with everyone (Romans 12:18).

And walk in the way of love, just as Christ loved us and gave himself up for us as a fragrant offering and sacrifice to God (Ephesians 5:2).

Your heavenly Father

CHAPTER 5

A Good Thing

Through my journey to love my husband in a way such as described in the Bible, there were many times I got discouraged. I realized I could not do it on my own. I was not made to be perfect, but I was made fearfully and wonderfully and would be an imperfect person under a perfect God. I faced so many challenges, such as feelings of discouragement, guilt, and frustration when I saw that seeking to be flawless in the way I expressed my love to my husband was not always going to be possible. There would be many times that I would mess up and make the wrong decisions. I had to remember that I had God to turn to and that I was a part of his plan and was one of his creations.

"I call on you, God, because you will answer me; listen closely to me, hear what I say" (Psalm 17:6). Have you ever felt like you have such a bad attitude, always messing up, and frustrated at little stuff, and just flat out feel unpeaceful? Have these emotions made you feel like you can't pray, or they just make you feel like you do not want to pray and you do not know why? God gave us his one and only son so we can have everlasting life. *Life!* A full life. Each day we face many things, and we have a choice. You can choose to cling to God and his word, or you can allow the day to cling to you weighing you down. Psalm 17:6 is powerful and is awesome reminder that when you call on God, he will listen and answer you. He already knows everything about you, including your many moods. There is nothing about you that God doesn't already know. The beauty of it is that he has shown us grace since the beginning of time.

I read the book of Genesis about the creation of the very first woman, the very first wife—Eve. When Adam's rib was taken to create Eve, his suitable helper, they were both naked. Their nakedness brings me to believe that Adam knew her. His knowledge of her was that God's creation was good, helpful, and there was no evil in her being. When the serpent came to tempt her, she gave in to her flesh and temptation, believing she would become more knowledgeable and wise and would eat what was attractive to her eyes. This action of hers caused consequences for women to face for years to come. It was then that their nakedness was exposed. Prior to the fall in the garden, they were transparent to each other, and there was nothing hidden in their marriage. Genesis 1:21 tells us, "that the Lord made for Adam and his wife garments of skins and clothed them." After reading that, I thought about how I'd messed up daily and how hard I had been on myself. We try so hard to hide our faults cause if we expose them, it is humiliating and brings about shame. We cannot hide in the garden forever from a God who made us and knows our every step. Genesis 1:21 shows a graceful God. He could have left them naked, but he covered them and went on to bless them with sons.

The enemy can try and come to you with lies about how your mistakes make you unfit to pray or radiate God's love. Know this: when the enemy comes, it is because he feels threatened that you are following the path God has for you. The enemy sees the blessings and fruit you bear that brings prosperity to your life. The enemy wants to throw rocks and thorns onto your path so you stumble. Just like Eve's sin and naked body were exposed, we should expose our faults and weaknesses so we may move forward and be accountable for our actions. Satan also likes to bring temptation our way. We must see it as temptation and see it as something we should strive to defeat. By seeking to defeat temptation, we give honor to God and defeat the enemy. We should step back from the temptation and see it for what it is. Live in wisdom, and live in prayer. We must pray and pray hard. God wants to talk to you and converse with you daily. How awesome it must have been for Adam and Eve to be in the Garden of Eden and walk with God daily, literally. God wants to get you through frustrations and obstacles. Ask God to help you each day and to take full control of your actions. I imagine a child sitting on a father's lap, whispering in his ear, while the father takes delight and smiles with patience and eagerness to help. Choose to walk with him each day.

In Genesis, there is much said about the first wife. It is written that it was not good for man to be alone, so he would make a helper suitable for man; he is referring to a wife. He saw all of his creation as good, but this one matter of a man being alone, he did not. I was fascinated by the word "suitable". God was saying that in marriage, as wives, we are suitable for the men to whom we are married. God's intention was for us to be helpers, suitable helpers. Another description I found of a wife that blessed me is in Proverbs 18:22 which says, "He who has found a wife has found a good thing." The term, "a good thing" will remain in my heart forever. I struggled so much every day, trying to be a reflection of God's love and failed many times, so when I saw that God saw me as "a good thing", I was determined to strive much more. All the bad attitudes, irritability, and frustrations I had did not make me the awful person I thought

I was, but it made me human. It made me an imperfect human being, falling short of the glory of God, as was his plan. I may glorify my God when I seek to be more like him and know that without him, not all things are possible.

We go about our days, having hope, whether we realize it or not. Our usual hopes consist of having a good day, good health, no traffic, a peaceful day at work, and calm kids. However, when we are well grounded in our walk with God and know we will strive to live according to his will, we have to understand that we fall short. It is times like those, we must be remember who we are in Christ. We must forgive ourselves as we seek forgiveness from our Father. There was a time when I wanted to work on having more patience with my husband while he was home. I would get frustrated as he sat on the couch, while I was constantly picking up toys. Once I got frustrated and lost my patience, I would get upset with him and upset with myself. I would tell God, "I guess I'm never going to get it right. I failed you again. I'm so sorry. I just don't know how to stay calm." It was a defeated feeling each time, but God reminded me that he hears me and that he knew my heart. He knew how hard I was trying, and he knew I would mess up even before I did. Our God sees the depths of our heart, and he still loves us. There was storm after storm, but God said after each of them that we would, always see a rainbow. After our storms, there is his covenant. "But those who hope in the Lord will renew their strength. They will soar on wings like eagles; they will run and not grow weary, they will walk and not be faint" (Isaiah 40:31) God brings strength and perseverance into our lives. When we walk with the Lord through our challenges and pain, we will not faint, but we will soar. We will soar, because we have the victory. The calling out to Jesus is not to summon him, because he will never leave us or forsake us, but it shows us his everlasting presence and his truth that sets us free, because he loved us first.

When I was a little girl, I was scared of thunder and lightning or those moving shadows that were caused by the trees outside on a windy night. I can still remember my heart pounding and being so terrified, I felt like I couldn't move. My dad always told me that when I got scared, I could call out to him, and he would come get me. So of course I would yell out, "Dad! Dad!" I would wait, sometimes he took a while and then I would yell again, "Dad! Dad!". This time he would come running to me, grab me, and hold me. He told me everything would be okay, and he had such gentleness as he rocked me back and forth. After he rescued me from my fears, he would begin to sing a song and rock me back to sleep. I will never forget the words.

"I love you with the love of the Lord,
I love you with the love of the Lord,
I can see it in your face, the glory of my king,
I love you with the love of the Lord"

He would sing it over and over until I fell asleep and was at peace. As the wife of a law enforcement officer, I often have to remind myself that I have a heavenly Father I can cry out to. I have a heavenly Father that never leaves me or forsakes me, but always comes when I call out his name: "Jesus! Jesus! Father!" When we hear of the loss of an officer, so many fears can arise; so many anxieties can surface. We are fearful of even thinking about losing our spouse. Many other fears can arise and bring about many fearful questions or scenarios. These questions can bring us to thinking, *What if something happens on duty? What will I do? What will happen to my family? Am I ready for something like that? Am I really appreciative of what I have? Do I take my family for granted? Am I living life to the fullest?* It is these times of fear, questions, and uncertainty that calling out the name of Jesus brings peace and calmness. Just like the song my father sang to me, there is something about the love of the Lord that just calms storms and brings about such amazing peace. There is something about his name that reminds us of how mighty he is and how small we are, yet although being small we are mighty women of God. The love of the Lord conquers all. It is seeing our God, looking at ourselves, and seeing the glory of our king. Seek to see his glory and his peace in your precious lives.

When we cry out to God, we are reminded of his presence and can see through our spiritual eyes. When we walk hand in hand with God through our life, and when we call on him, he just lets go of our hand and carries us the rest of the way. We serve a God who delights in his children and who wants only prosperity in their lives. We were created and knitted together to live on this earth for such a time as this. Our journey as an officer's wife is no mistake. It was not a chance that you took or that God took. We are called to be the helpers, the suitable helpers, to the sons of God. Their line of work is a calling, and as wives, we are called to duty as well. Your days were preordained, and it is important to ask God to fulfill his will in your life and especially your marriage. You are the daughters of a king and hold such amazing favor. When I look back to all the struggles I had, and I understand that I will face struggles in the future, I can't help but smile that God cares about my role as a wife, and he says I am a good thing. You are a good thing! Our God has the best ideas and the greatest creations. He created the wife.

He created marriage, and his plan for it was good and was to be the expression of Christ's love for the church. Honor your role and remember that you are a delight in your Father's eye. There are no surprises for God. He sees ahead and simply wants us to leave our future in his hands so he can carry out his perfect will that prospers you. God does not call the perfect; he calls the willing. The mantle you wear and carry is one that God has saved to allow a special person to bear. So bear it with great honor unto him, for you are the chosen one. He will honor you greatly in the process. You have the favor of the Lord.

We will face many storms in this life. There will be times when someone may come and rain on your parade, but it is up to you whether that person will dictate the outcome of your parade, or if you will be prepared and ready to open your umbrella of protection. Following God is such a blessing, and it is something that is to be honored. When we follow God, we become his child. As a child of God, we hold favor and blessings as long as we seek him. Life can bring goodness, but it can also bring trial and tribulation. It can bring storms. In these trials we face, we have two choices: we can fall on our knees in prayer, or we can grow bitterness, fear, discouragement, and anger in our hearts, causing us to give up. James 1:2-4 it says, "Consider it pure joy, my brothers, whenever you face trials of many kinds, because you know that the testing of your faith develops perseverance. Perseverance must finish its work so that you may be mature and complete, not lacking anything." This Scripture is awesome because it lets you know why trials or storms can be such a blessing. Choose to cling to God when facing any storm, so he can guide you and grow you spiritually. In trials, he wants perseverance to become a part of you. You can do all things through Christ who strengthens you. You can come out of any storm soaked with hurt and pain, but then God's light will fall upon you, and you just stand in stillness, drying off all that has been inflicted and simply stand in light and peace. Simply stand in the presence of your almighty God. After a storm, we always see the sun come out, the calmness, and the rainbow running across the sky. It is beautiful and breathtaking to see. The calmness after the storm is when God is so glorified. Joy does come in the morning. Joy does come to those who seek him. When you seek him, you will want to glorify him.

Matthew 24:35 says "Heaven and earth will pass away, but my words will never pass away." God gave us his word to use as a stepping stone, as guidance, or as an umbrella to shield you from your storms. God loves you so much and just wants you to surrender all your trials to him, so he can bring you out of your storm, matured, complete, lacking nothing, and radiating God's beautiful glory. He wants you to live in abundance. Storms will come. You can look at them as dreary and depressing, or you can look at them as beautiful—a beautiful storm where God is glorified, and out of the ashes, you rise. Our joy is found in the Lord. God made all things, and all of it is good. You are good and are an original masterpiece. Every single feature on you was made, carefully, perfectly, and wonderfully. Each day that we leave in his hands will bring our goodness and brings our victory.

REFLECTION

How do you view your role as an officer's wife?

Is your marriage something you see as ordained by the Lord?

After reading Genesis and Proverbs, have you ever seen yourself with such value as the wife of an officer?

How do you view yourself in Christ? Do you see yourself through the eyes of God?

Read Psalm 139:13-14 Write this Scripture, and read it to yourself every day. Begin to see yourself through God's eyes.

Father,

I cannot tell you how much I rejoice over your unfailing love for me. I love that you delight in me and see me as a good thing. I pray that I will better understand what it means to be a suitable helper. I ask that I would see myself though your eyes and forgive myself when needed. I trust that your grace is new each day and is sufficient. I pray to feel your everlasting presence in my heart and as I go through each day. Help me to remember how fearfully and wonderfully made I am. I pray that in all things, I will know that as long as you are with me, I can do all things. Help me to be graceful in all I do and that I will bring a smile to your face. You are my Father, my redeemer, my healer, and my strength. Thank you, Lord, for loving me first and loving me with such a great love that I cannot comprehend.

In Jesus' name,
Amen.

TRUTH

_____,

(write your name above)

"I call on you, God, because you will answer me; listen closely to me, hear what I say" (Psalm 17:6).

And we know that in all things, God works for the good of those who love him, who have been called according to his purpose (Romans 8:28).

Therefore, my brothers and sisters, make every effort to confirm your calling and election. For if you do these things, you will never stumble (2 Peter 1:10).

I praise you because I am fearfully and wonderfully made; your works are wonderful, I know that full well (Psalm 139:14).

Your heavenly Father

Chaplain Allison P. Uribe

CHAPTER 6

His Glory

This journey was turning into a passion of mine as time went by. I surrendered my life and marriage to God, I sought his will, I learned about who I was in Christ and what it meant, and now I wanted to glorify him. Glorifying God is not something to consider as work but to consider as a natural response. God had done many good works in my life and in my marriage, and I could not keep silent about it. It was such an inner joy that was meant for release and all in due time. I wanted to share my testimony with others and wanted to do this in hope that many would see that the impossible is always possible with God. It was a surrender to give this life that was given to me and move forward to believe in a God who still moves all to victory.

My husband was not a church-going man, yet neither was I in the beginning years of our marriage. Through seeking God and changing my ways to his way, I began to see the fruit that was borne from it. Living my life as a witness to the word won the heart of my husband. It was not me who changed my husband; it was God in me and his mighty hand. I had this promise in the book of Peter. "Wives, in the same way be submissive to your husbands so that, if any of them do not believe the word, they may be won over without words by the behavior of their wives, when they see the purity and reverence of your lives" (1Peter 3:1-2). When I read that verse, it does not say to me that we must always be silent; it says that we must choose our words wisely and choose to give it to God, who can move mountains. Our God is mighty to save all things, and that is just what he did. I remained faithful to what I vowed to do as a wife and focused on my God, who loved me first. I strived to be joyful and remain in Christ, so I could radiate just that. After attending church for a while, my husband, who had not been attending, finally went to church. My husband wanted what I had, and I had God at the center of my heart. I didn't have to nag him or constantly remind him that we needed to go to church. Instead, I just showed him with my actions the importance of having a Christ-centered marriage. I made myself a willing vessel to be used for the Lord. I knew that if my husband and I attended church, and we were to live out our lives with God, amazing promises would be fulfilled, and our family would live in abounding love and grace for all eternity. Church was now a part of our household. To this day, I am so amazed at how God has truly transformed our household and our marriage. Church was and is our top priority, and after years of flourishing in our marriage and in our walk, I couldn't be silent anymore.

I was at a mall, window shopping, when a woman walked toward me. I assumed she was another shopper, but then she smiled hesitantly and said, "Excuse me." She looked at me in a state of disbelief and told me she felt the need to talk to me. She apologized for the intrusion and then said that although we knew nothing about each other, she wanted me to know that she was having marital issues. Many thoughts went running through my mind, and in my heart, I knew this was no accident. It was a divine appointment and an opportunity for me to glorify God for his holy works. I assured her that it was okay that she had approached me and that I would listen to her story. She proceeded to tell me that her spouse had run off with another woman and was seeking a divorce. She cried, saying that she loved him so much, and divorce was something she did not want. She wanted to believe they would somehow reconcile. I wanted to tell her about what God had done for me, but I knew I needed simply to listen. She repeatedly said that she felt all be would be well, but she was not sure what it meant. It was then that I told her about my marriage, without offering too much detail. My marriage had its struggles, but I could not relate to her situation in any way. I simply asked her one question. I asked if she was a person who prayed and had a belief in God. She looked at me with such a straight face and seemed uncertain of how to reply. She said she had not prayed about it but that she would start to. I told her how important it was to leave it in God's hands and that when I did, God transformed my marriage. At the time, I was still timid about praying in public or even with someone. However, I knew there was reason God had placed us together. I took the deepest breath and asked her if I could pray with her. Her face was priceless. She looked surprised but gladly accepted. I found myself surprised as well, as we stood in the middle of a mall, with many people passing by. It took courage on my part to stand there and pray in the middle of the mall. It was out of my comfort zone, but in my heart, I knew that is what God wanted me to do. Once we finished our prayer, I gave her a big hug and told her I would continue to pray for her and knew God would do something great.

After that day, I prayed that God would take this life of mine and make me a vessel to do his work here on earth. I wanted to testify and encourage other women. Then, he did the unimaginable.

As the days went on and months went by, I found myself in many situations or should I say, divine appointments. Women came to me to talk about their marital issues. The neat thing about this was that no one really knew my marriage had suffered. Sure, some people knew there was a disagreement here and there, but they had no idea I was unhappy at one point in my marriage. I saw this as God's allowing me to be a blessing and giving me opportunities to glorify him. I loved being able to witness for Christ and give women hope. Ministering to women made me hunger for more opportunity. I went into deep prayer to find out exactly what I was seeking and how I could continuously testify. Of course, anyone can testify and minister, but I felt it was deeper than that. I looked back to the many years of struggle, praying, and the freedom I found in God. I kept thinking, though, that the whole time I struggled, there was not one person who ever understood. I was a law enforcement wife but didn't know any other law enforcement wives. It finally made sense to me as to why I felt alone all that time. Our marriages are so unique and hold so many different challenges that only another law enforcement wife could understand. It then hit me, there had to be more law enforcement wives out there who felt the way I did or who were struggling. I thought it would be so great if maybe about four or five officers' wives could join me for a Bible study or just get together for prayer or fellowship. I had no idea where to start, and so my prayers geared toward wisdom and guidance. I shared my ideas for ministering to officers' wives with my husband, and he encouraged it. There was only one problem: I didn't know anyone.

After a year passed, with many more ministering opportunities, I decided to talk to my church about this idea. The pastor supported it, and by then, I had so many ideas, and plans, and a vision in my heart. The pastor knew only one other woman in the church who was married to an officer, but that filled me with joy. It was a start. My pastor gave me some homework; he said to come up with a mission statement and a name for what would be a small group in my church. This was so exciting! I finally felt like I could move forward. I prayed about a name for days but still had no idea what to call my group. The funny thing is that I took so long with trying to figure out a name, but then when I asked my husband if he had any ideas, he just blurted out, "Wives on Duty." I had never been so excited! It was perfect and so funny that he got it on the first try. So now I had the name Wives on Duty and a mission to go out and support and encourage wives of law enforcement, fire department, and emergency services personnel through the word of God.

I had one wife as a member, but it did not matter, because I knew God put me to this work. A couple of years went by, and one wife grew into two, and then two grew into five, and five grew into forty-five, and now, there are almost too many to count. Getting to those numbers was a hard lesson. God gives and blesses if he knows we will take care of what he has given. "And we know that in all things God works for the good of those who love him and have been called according to his purpose" (Romans 8:28). Although I had one member at the gatherings the majority of the time, it was God who had asked me if I would care for her. It was a time for me to show him that he could trust me and know that I would care for her heart with grace and gentleness. For example, when our family eats dinner, we don't necessarily bring out the fine china. If we have company or someone we are trying to impress, we bring out the fancier dishes and show more proper behavior at the dinner table. Why is that? Does our family deserve any less? It is not about bringing out your fine dishes every night, but it is about treating and caring for what is considered our gift, as is fitting to the Lord. We should uphold our blessings. Our fine china should be the grace and love we express to our family. All that he brings our way, we should treat with care and treat all people as if we are doing it for the Lord. Let everything for which you put your hands to work glorify God.

There were times when I wanted to give up, because there were so many voices of defeat around me. I saw with my physical eyes and not my spiritual eyes. God had an ordained time for this ministry, and in each of our lives, there is a time and purpose for all things. It wasn't about numbers anymore, which had been an insecurity on my part for far too long. It was about what I was going to do with the numbers I had. I put my faith into action and cared for each wife that God brought my way, as was fitting to the Lord.

Since the ministry began, God has blessed Wives on Duty in so many amazing ways, and he has enabled me to minister to wives nationally. This could be considered a calling, but the way I see it, there was a need, and I was willing. I promised God to meet that need to glorify him. Each day holds a ministry opportunity. From the moment we wake up in the morning to the moment we go to sleep, if we are alert and are open to hear his voice and the prompting of the Holy Spirit, God will move in such a way that answers prayer and exalts him. We go about our days with free will, but in the end, God already has ordained our days, and our comings and goings are really in his mighty hands. He is a God who has full control and is ready to make our paths straight when we get off track. God does not use the qualified; he uses the willing. As wives, we must seek to have a willing spirit and allow ourselves to be used to glorify him. One way to show a willing spirit is by prayer. Praying with a prayer of unshakeable faith over your spouse shows your willingness to have faith, to know God is at work, and to have victory in your circumstances. It is a question of what you are willing to do in your daily lives that will glorify the kingdom of God. Glorifying him is something that should come naturally because of all of his goodness and richness. Wake up each day and see the many blessings – that is reason enough to glorify him and praise him in all circumstances. The sun that shines upon you radiates his glory and is so beautiful to see. When we glorify God in our home and in our marriage, imagine the beauty that will radiate in your lives and to those around you. It is being a witness through your actions. The majority of the time, your actions minister to others, and your actions are far more powerful than words could ever be. We must put all pride aside and take up the cross. We will receive our blessing in obedience to what he has called us to, in this role as an officer's wife. Let nothing hinder you from doing the Lord's work, and let nothing rob you of the blessing upon your marriage.

Serving Christ is a natural response for those who seek him—a service that brings the love of God to those in need. Many people, including our very own families, are lost, broken, rejected, angry, prejudiced, hateful, and bound by addictions of the world. But what does it really mean? We all sin and fall short of the glory of God. When we are called as helpers, we not only show them love and compassion, but we help them remove the worldly glasses that prevent them from seeing through their spiritual eyes and seeing the worth of their life. As wives we can show the beauty that can't be seen and excel in Christ so we can try to understand what we cannot explain—not because we don't know it, but because it is too amazing for words. When those dear to us cannot see the glory of God and his purpose, how amazing the task to describe and bring them to a God who is indescribable. We can be a vessel for him in his work, to bring our loved ones to a new beginning and into many victorious moments in their lives. Our Father has the vision, and we wait upon him for instruction to see that the vision is carried out. We share a success, but we do not obtain it, because it was not ours but his. In our own walk with God, we should not, at any time, find ourselves looking down on others and where they are in their walk with the Lord. This is especially vital in our marriage. We should be graceful enough to express Christ-like behavior without condemning our spouse, who may be lost. We all fall short; we cannot judge others, based on our own convictions or look down on others by seeing ourselves as above all that. We cannot push our own convictions on others! It is not for us to correct or to convict but God's and in his time.

Serving is a giving of ourselves to be the salt and light, so our God can use us to bring this to a hurting world. Of course we should bring salt and light into our first ministry, our home. If we can't serve without holding expectations of others, then what good is it to serve? We must seek to do such things as a servant of God, but we must also seek to protect all God has given us. To protect and serve is protecting God, our children, our homes, and our marriages. It is obeying the authority of our God and being a reverent wife. Being a servant of God and being a helper to our spouse also makes us his friend. As a friend, we must seek what we can do in our friendship with him. We must see that friends talk to each other, depend on each other, trust, respect, love, and show service. As we depend on God, he depends on us. He too depends on our obedience and our willingness, and this knowledge should take us to new heights and the way we see our calling as a wife on duty.

"Where two or three are gathered in my name, there I am in the midst of them" (Matthew 18:20). This awesome power is brought when we are gathered because he dwells with us. Calling on him does not bring him to us, because he is already there. Calling on him allows us to gain sight, and it peels back the things we do not see in the spiritual. What will that mean to us, as wives of law enforcement? Wives on Duty was not formed to fail but to excel. It excels as we, as wives, choose to fight for our marriages so we may not fall into the traps of the enemy. The traps will allow Satan to rob our families of the unity and joy that comes with being a portrait of God's beautiful creation, the family. Our failure as a group of law enforcement wives does not depend on others or circumstances that surround us through divorce and broken families. It depends solely on us and the free will to view it as a failure. For example, when running a marathon, does the runner view his winning based on who is running or based on his run alone? This is where prayer must be said in order for us to move forward and yet be attentive to the traps of the enemy. There may be many disappointments from others we are close to—friends, our church, our children, and our spouse—but it is not for us to be disappointed. How much more of a disappointment is it to God, before whom we all fall short? Who are we to have people meet expectations that we set, when we can't come close to meeting those of our Father?

Being a helpmeet goes beyond serving. It is a surrender of life, pride, and selfish ambition. As we take pride in our roles, we must not see ourselves as a success but as a workmanship of God, who shines because of the obedience we live by to glorify him. We must seek to be made more in his image. As time goes on, our salt may lose its taste, but when we remove ourselves from the worldly view of how we are to be as women, we will see that it is a surrender and expression—not what friends or talk shows have told us we should be. We are simply to be the hands and feet of Christ. We are to excel in his calling. This is not to say that we do the work on this earth to glorify. It is the willingness in our heart that allows the Holy Spirit to flow through us. Allowing the Holy Spirit to flow though us will be the true blessing toward others, especially in our homes. It is God's holy works and not ours. This will give us a calm knowledge that all we encounter are helped by the spirit that flows through us. "Whatever you do, work at it with all your heart as working for the Lord and not for man" (Colossians 3:23). When protecting our home, marriage, ourselves, and others, which falls under God's authority, we must not do this for man but for our God. It is a show of reverence and a servant's heart. In all things, we must seek wisdom and ready ourselves before our day begins. As wives on duty, we must be ready to assist in advancing our husband and homes in the kingdom of God and into their blessings and victory. We must not see those whom we help as work, but as a divine appointment. You must care for whatever God has placed in your path. How much effort will you give to something ordained by the Lord? Dwelling with God and desiring only his will and his work will allow his spirit to flow through you and into the lives of many, beginning in your home. We must be equipped and look at our home, our work, and our goals as a step closer to bringing our home to Christ in wisdom and in knowledge. Moving forward in your ministry at home should not be considered extra work but as a mission; not a burden but a pleasure. It's time to complete the vision and do it with Christ, who strengthens us. Be the wife on duty who fights the fight and wins with Christ!

We can glorify God though our actions, or we can glorify him through praise. "Sing to him, sing praises to him, speak of all his wonders" (1 Corinthians 16:9). Praise to our God can be the strongest weapon to overcome our trials and tribulations. Praise is said to be our strength in times of trouble. The purpose and importance of praise is to celebrate the victory that we already are promised by a mighty God who is worthy of praise. We praise him for all he has done in previous trials and how great he is to supply our every need. Praise is an expression of our love and gratitude and can be done in many ways—there is no correct way. It is a time of fellowship with him and our one-on-one time, speaking with him. It may not necessarily mean a time to ask him for things or present our trials but it is a proclaiming of his promises in our trials and praising him that because his word stands true, all is well.

When it comes to praise, I like to think of a child, seeing his father and raising his arms up in joy and asking to be held. The significance of raising his arms is a surrender of self and saying, "I do not want to stand alone. I want you to hold me, help me, and carry me through." This is expressed in joy or in sadness but ultimately, it ends in joy. When we praise God, our confidence in God brings us to know that with him, all things are possible, and all things work out for the good of those who love him. His name is greatly to be praised, not only for the victory that it brings but for the magnificence it holds. Praising and glorifying him is something he delights in. As wives of officers, praise should be a part of our daily routine. We should have an attitude of gratitude. There is much to be thankful for and much to praise.

REFLECTION

What has God spoken to you when it comes to your home, marriage, children, or workplace?

When going about your daily activities, do you ever wonder if all you do is done to glorify God?

If God asked you to step out of your comfort zone in order to glorify him, what would you do? Why?

Make a list. What ways can you think of that will glorify God in your home and in your marriage?

Father,

In my heart I know your love, goodness, and mercy will follow me all the days of my life. I praise you for that. I pray that all I do in this life will be to glorify you. Help me to glorify you in my marriage and in my home. Give me a boldness to step out of my comfort zone and advance the kingdom of God. I pray that while my husband serves and protects our city, you will place his feet where needed and that he, too, will glorify you to those who are lost, broken, and hurting. Forgive me if my actions do not display your love to others. I want to be more like you and yearn to see through my spiritual eyes. Help me to put my faith into action.

In Jesus' name,
Amen.

TRUTH

_____,

(write your name above)

But seek his kingdom, and these things will be given to you as well (Luke 12:31).

Do not focus on what is seen but what is unseen (2 Corinthians 4:18).

Whatever you do, work at it with all your heart, as working for the Lord, not for human masters (Colossians 3: 23).

Give thanks in all circumstances; for this is God's will for you in Christ Jesus (1 Thessalonians 5:18).

But I have raised you up for this very purpose, that I might show you my power and that my name might be proclaimed in all the earth (Exodus 9:16).

Your heavenly Father

CHAPTER 7

The Enemy I Laugh At

Once we have an understanding of who we are in Christ and how we will continue to be on the winning side, we must understand that where there is good, there also is evil. In Ephesians, it clearly states that we battle not against flesh and blood but against principalities in the heavenlies. There is a continuous spiritual battle going on, and for the most part, we are unaware of it. The battle includes those thoughts of defeat and discouragement when we are already feeling down; when we find ourselves battling to obtain joy with our spouse, but all he has ever done wrong keeps coming to your mind and consuming you. I faced many times in my marriage and in the beginning of the ministry when I knew there was a battle to be fought and won because of who I served.

After the birth of my first two children, my marriage, although doing well, felt unfruitful. I went about my days, doing my daily chores—cleaning, washing, caring for the children, and cooking—and seeking a break or some quiet time. My husband would return home from work, tired from the day, and although I understood he needed to rest a bit before he could help, many thoughts came to mind. I wondered why he couldn't tough it out and just not nap, or I'd think about how I never got one break, yet I allowed him to have one. It was like a day-to-day rerun with no progress. Of course, God was advancing us in many ways, but it was days like those that kept me from moving forward, because I allowed those thoughts to take over. If I was not careful, those thoughts would begin to consume me. It led me to feel sorry for myself—to feel defeated and useless. Of course, these things were not true, and there were many times that I became so angry that I could not pray. I was consumed with a spirit of anger. One thing I would forget to do was to arm myself with the armor of God, first thing in the morning. "Put on all of God's armor so that you will be able to stand firm against all strategies of the devil" (Ephesians 6:11). When we wake up in the morning, we forget so often what a blessing it is to just open our eyes and see. We forget to be grateful for the present. We also forget to invite God to take control of our day and to leave it all in his hands. One of the many prayer requests is to ask that we obtain the full armor of God.

What does the armor of God consist of? You will find that in Ephesians 6:10-18.

Finally, be strong in the Lord and in his mighty power. Put on the full armor of God, so that you can take your stand against the devil's schemes. For our struggle is not against flesh and blood, but against the rulers, against the authorities, against the powers of this dark world and against the spiritual forces of evil in the heavenly realms. Therefore put on the full armor of God, so that when the day of evil comes, you may be able to stand your ground, and after you have done everything, to stand. Stand firm then, with the belt of truth buckled around your waist, with the breastplate of righteousness in place, and with your feet fitted with the readiness that comes from the gospel of peace. In addition to all this, take up the shield of faith, with which you can extinguish all the flaming arrows of the evil one. Take the helmet of salvation and the sword of the Spirit, which is the word of God. And pray in the Spirit on all occasions with all kinds of prayers and requests. With this in mind, be alert and always keep on praying for all the Lord's people."

Let's dissect this verse and go back to the beginning of how each piece of armor will give us a victorious day and lead us into victorious living as a wife on duty. It begins with speaking of the belt of truth—the truth being the word of God—and in making our speech truthful, and in speaking of wisdom. This is so important when we find ourselves feeling defeated, depressed, angry, or consumed with the many emotions the day or our lives bring. With the word of God engraved in our hearts, we can stand against such emotions or what we see as impossible situations. It gives us a chance to walk by faith and not by sight. During those times of discouragement in my marriage—once I mastered the true meaning of obtaining the armor—I was able to move on and bear its fruit. When I felt a spirit of anger coming on I would speak 2 Timothy 1:7 and say that I was not made of a spirit of anger but of joy, peace, and sound mind. This was something I would continue to do until I felt a release and peace. When the word of God becomes a part of our lives we are able to face the lie with truth and stand on God's word. As wives on duty, we must be geared up with the word of truth and be able to acknowledge the power it holds, because of the power our God has when we speak it in faith. When we have the truth in us, we are able to walk by faith, because what we see daily or in the circumstances we face, we know it can be transformed in the hands of God. It's important to take time during the day to read at least a paragraph in your Bible or write down a Scripture and post it on your fridge. By doing this, you prepare yourself for any circumstance and add truth to your belt. In a previous chapter, I spoke of the Sam Brown, which is the gun belt our husband's wear on duty. We also can apply that same concept to the belt of truth. The belt is full of tools to meet the needs of an officer. The gun is used to target the enemy and to do harm before harm is done to the officer. The bullets are like the truth that pierces into the enemy to win the battle that is already guaranteed to be won. The flashlight is used to expose and to reveal the enemy, even when we do not see it ahead. The cuffs are to bind the enemy and his attempts, so his tactics may not further. When you see this vital equipment from now on, you will see that the battles our husband face daily are against such evils of the world; they truly are the sons of God.

The next part of the armor of God is the breastplate of righteousness. We must seek to live in righteousness. This means we must do our best to live free of guilt, avoid falling into sin, and be justifiable. We all fall short of God's glory, but that does not excuse us to live in sin and blame it on that. God knows the depths of our heart and delights in those who seek to do his will and try their best to obtain it. For example, when we make New Year's resolutions, we make them believing we will be successful, but most people believe only for a short time. By mid-year, their hopes to better their lives are a thing of the past, and they give up. We must not give up when it comes to walking righteously with God. How great the blessing to those who persevere to the end. Let us keep a clear conscious, all the while protecting our hearts and minds from sinful things. Righteousness is very important in our law enforcement homes. We must live this in our homes to help guide our families as they go out each day and face the world. Our husbands on duty have access to money, drugs, stolen property, flirtatious women, and much more. How can we not walk in righteousness so that we may be able to stand in prayer before God and have nothing to hinder our requests to protect our husband's integrity and flesh? There are many spirits of greed, temptation, lust, and anger out there that we cannot afford not to seek first God's kingdom. This seeking of righteousness will equip us so that in the time of trial, we can face it head on for what it is.

As we head onto face our victories, we must remember that our feet should be fitted with the readiness from the gospel of peace. Each day we awake, as we ask the Lord to arm us with the full armor of God, we must ask that our steps be ordained. This could be a prayer, seeking God to lead us on the paths of righteousness, controlling our comings and goings, bringing us to those to whom we can be a blessing, and seeking our preordained days to come to pass. As wives, we can remember this as we lift our husband's up in prayer. We can ask God to send our husbands to the calls where they need to be, to guide their steps on duty, and to keep them from harm. When we seek God's will in our lives, we also can seek to be a blessing to others. Being ready with the gospel of peace in our hearts will allow us to speak life into others and to know the truth in our hearts, so when we face evil, we will be ready to face our giants head on and walk into our victory. The Lord knows our every move and holds our every moment in this life. With our feet grounded in his word and walking in truth, we cannot fall but will rise up each time. As flowers are planted in the ground, the roots require water, nutrients, sun, and good soil to grow and flourish. We are like flowers planted in this world, needing the water of life—his word. We also need our feet, our hearts, and our spirit to be full of his truth and his light and to be grounded in good soil, which can be righteousness. Be careful where you set foot each day. You must observe with whom you choose to surround yourself and where you allow your feet to take you. Are your feet walking on the right path?

As you ready yourself to ground your feet in the gospel of peace, be prepared to face your day with the shield of faith. It says in Ephesians that the shield of faith can extinguish all the flaming arrows of the evil one. When we walk in faith and not by sight, because we know the truth, we can quickly recognize the tactics of the enemy. The enemy can try to bring so much doubt and fear our way that if we allow it to consume us, we then may fall into the traps and believe in defeat. With the shield of faith, we can walk head on to our circumstance, focusing on God and not allowing any doubt or fear to enter our hearts. For example, when a rhinoceros gets covered in dirt, it is so thick-skinned that the dirt dries up and falls right off. Our shield of faith is much the same—when the enemy throws his schemes our way we must be ready to throw our truth right back, allowing his lies to dry up and fade away.

Next, we have the helmet of salvation and the sword of the spirit, which is the word of God. We also are called to pray in the spirit on all occasions and always keep praying for the Lord's people. As we gear up with the armor of God, we walk about our day ready, ready to face the daily challenges. It can set the outcome of the day when we pray to be armed with such greatness and power. The word of God stands true and is the same today, tomorrow, and always. As we know the word in our hearts, it can help us to pray for others and hope that they, too, will seek the Lord's will in their lives. We plant seeds of greatness and allow God to grow it exceedingly well. Even if we face people with whom we don't get along or who are miserable and unfriendly, we can simply display Christ's love, without ever having to say a word. When you are equipped with the armor of God, as it protects you, it also brings about radiance in you. Have you ever met a person who just radiates when he or she enters a room? It is Christ in them that radiates. We should seek to hold such radiance in our homes and in those who surrounded us. When we equip ourselves, we become a blessing in ways unimaginable. A living blessing can be a smile to a woman who may be feeling depressed, allowing someone to go ahead of you in traffic, doing something nice for the woman at work that no one likes, or showing grace to the person who says awful things about law enforcement officers. It is all a choice when we wake up each day. The sword of the spirit, God's word, is our ultimate weapon in all things. Our salvation in Christ is something no one can take away.

As I looked back on this Scripture, I thought of a police officer's uniform. They gear up each day for battle in the cities they serve and protect. Their breastplate of righteousness is their Kevlar vest; their belt of truth is their gun belt. Their feet are grounded in boots, and this is like being grounded in the gospel of peace; their sword of the spirit is their gun, ready to shoot out the enemy. These men go out each day facing such evils and should be honored for it. I commend those who seek the Lord as a law enforcement officer. These sons of God seek their Father. How beautiful it is to know who their help comes from. Our help comes from the Maker of heaven and earth. How can we not turn to him in all we face?

Years ago when I started Wives on Duty, the attendance was low and it seemed no one had interest. It was then that I had to equip myself with the truth. I had many people tell me that maybe I should just stick with a support group and not make it such a "God thing." I laughed it off! My thought was this: "Why am I going to take God out of what is his to begin with?" I know he called me to this ministry, and therefore, everything about it will all be about him. It was a choice I made to stand in his word and to believe that God would see me through whatever came my way as a leader. Many women came and went throughout the years, and I knew if I stayed faithful and focused on what God saw for this ministry, the vision would come to pass. As I look back, I do laugh. I laugh at the enemy who tried to tell me that more people would come if it wasn't such a "God thing." As wives on duty, we must be ready to laugh at the enemy and his tactics. Many people fear the devil, but not I. The Lord gave us a spirit of joy, and a spirit of peace, and spirit of sound mind. How can we not live a life of laughter when we have the victory in Christ? When you wake up each day, I challenge you to smile immediately. Beginning the day with a smile, a prayer of thanksgiving, and then asking to be equipped with the armor of God can only lead you into a whole new level in Christ. Our joy in the Lord shall be our strength.

The high divorce rate among couples in this line of work is so sad, but I refuse to look at those statistics in the wrong way. The right way to look at the statistics is to believe you will not be part of it, that you do not expect it to increase, and that you believe it will decrease. I am stepping out in faith to believe that law enforcement will be known for its increase in saved marriages. As we face the many unique challenges in our marriages, we must remember that we do not battle flesh and blood; we battle against the darkness of the evil one. I put this faith into action a few times, and it was almost comical. If I ever found myself in a disagreement with my spouse, I would sometimes remember to apply that Scripture and look at it as a battle with the enemy and not my spouse. It was not easy at times, but I would quickly recognize the anger beginning to build up, and I would turn it around. If my spouse got me upset, I would go to him and do something nice or go out of my way to make him laugh, so we would both laugh. It was throwing love toward evil. This was so worth doing. There were many times that joy was chosen over an argument, and the blessings of that were astounding. I was being bold in the Lord. We must be bold in the Lord for the sake of our marriages. We must recognize that the enemy is defeated and that his tactics are merely attempts and do not prosper in any way, shape, or form unless we allow it. Isaiah 54:17 says, "No weapon formed against you shall prevail, and you will refute every tongue that accuses you." I just love that verse. This is why I am able to laugh at the enemy. The devil can try, but he never succeeds when we have a mighty God who has given us victory and joy.

Live to laugh, wives on duty. This life is so short and so precious that we might just miss the richness of life if we choose to live it in defeat. Times may get tough, and we may feel alone in our marriages or in other areas of our lives, but laughter and joy in the Lord will be our strength. Knowing we battle things in the heavenlies should not keep us still but keep us ready to fight for our marriages and our children. We must look at the enemy head on and tell him boldly that he will not come in and take our family, our home, or our children. We must take a stand as wives of law enforcement officers and see to it that we maintain a home that is full of laughter, where God is at the center. We know our husbands go out and face such darkness; let's fight to keep our homes a safe and peaceful refuge for our spouses to live in. Let us also not forget to pray! We also can pray with prayers of faith and in declaration. How can we do this? We can pray aloud and speak out God's word into our lives with an unshakeable faith. Remember, we may face daily battles and challenges in our marriages, but they are already our victory when we leave them with God. There was a time when I felt very down and depressed. I called on others to pray for me during that time, as I found myself unable to pray. Well, those prayers were answered, as they always are, because my depression went into battle. I began to look at the situation through my spiritual eyes and became angry that so many thoughts of defeat were in my head and consuming me. I figured it was the enemy, trying to keep me down and keep me from enjoying my every-day blessings. Prayer holds such amazing power that it can release us from all things in which we are bound or release us from the pit we dug for ourselves. The toughest battle I faced was healing from an incident that occurred when I was a child. When I was in second grade, my teacher was pregnant, and we knew that she would be out for a long while as she took maternity leave. As any child would be, we were all excited to have a substitute—someone different from our teacher. The arrival of my teacher's baby came, and we had a male substitute who also was a pastor. We students had thought the time with a substitute teacher would be exciting and fun, but it was not. After a few weeks of having our substitute, he began to touch me in inappropriate ways. I was molested, and at the time, I had no idea how to find safety or even expose his behavior. I had no idea what was happening to me at the time; all I knew was that I was uncomfortable, felt sick, felt fear, and felt alone. I recall many times when I would look across at the principal's office and wondered if I should just run and scream. But each time I stayed quiet and stood still; I was unable to move. A few more weeks passed. I was at gymnastics, and I remember seeing my mother come in with tears in her eyes. She grabbed me and took me outside, apologizing for not knowing. The substitute teacher also had molested my best friend, and the police were at her house, taking a report. I remember thinking it was finally over. It was now out in the open, and I could finally breathe. As I look back to that, it brings pain and anger. Maybe it was then that I found myself in a pit that I had not made for myself. Although it felt as if it was over at that very moment, I realized it was not. I carried that throughout my life, not ever wanting to face it but instead talked about it as if it was not a big deal. Each time I felt angry about it or allowed myself to drown in pity and anger, I made the pit even deeper. I had an anger toward men and thought of them as dirty and selfish for their own sexual desires. It is easier for us to brush our hurts under the rug than to expose them and face them head on. Because intimacy was a part of marriage, this brought conflict. I knew I needed healing so that I could stop being quiet, as I had done as a little girl. Knowing God has helped me to be forgiving and to allow God to heal all areas of my life. It was in this area of my marriage that God would turn whatever the enemy meant for harm into joy and in my favor. How? I asked God to heal me of this pain and to free me from it. Intimacy is a gift God has given us as married couples, to enjoy and to take pleasure in. I found myself struggling in this, and my husband's touch was something I had to have control over. I viewed intimacy as a bad and dirty thing and something not to be discussed. Each time he tried to reach out for me, I would brush him off or even walk away to avoid it. I recall a time that my husband came up behind me in the kitchen to give me a kiss and be flirtatious. I told him, "Honey, we just came back from church." He looked at me, surprised and confused, and said, "But you're my wife." When he said that, I knew that I was only partly healed. I still viewed touch and intimacy as a dirty thing. Our husbands' touch and desire to be with us is such a blessing, but we can be robbed of that if we have been hurt by molestation or any other past sexual hurts. I had to face it again, head on, for what it was—an unhealed wound. I felt as if the gift given to me was taken away, ruined and then handed back to me. What a lie the enemy had told me! Of course God did not pull me out of the pit I was in immediately, but he did sit in it with me, and slowly, together, the both of us have climbed out. As hard as it was and is to this day, I find a peace in praying for the one who caused me such harm. I pray for the substitute teacher who molested me years ago, and when I pray for him, I ask God to help me see through my spiritual eyes and to be graceful. I pray for this man to seek the Lord and that he seeks forgiveness. Forgiving him does not justify what he did, but it has allowed me to feel free and to rise out of those ashes. I know I have a long journey of healing ahead, but for now, I have found a peace and joy in praying for him. "But I tell you, love your enemies and pray for those who persecute you" (Matthew 5:44). My answer to healing from my hurt and my heart is by living out God's command in the book of Matthew. This has enabled me to laugh at the enemy and his many attempts to keep me bound in those moments I faced in the second-grade classroom. I refuse to allow what the enemy meant for harm to keep harming me. I will continue, however, to give it to God, and allow him to turn it into good, and give me my beauty for those ashes. The Bible holds many promises that can set us free. We should declare his word and make it known to the enemy that he has no authority. The only way I knew how to express it was to write out the truth I knew in my heart and throw it in the enemy's face.

Satan,

I write this in hopes that you will fully understand my commitment to God and his faithfulness to me. You have come into my thoughts and twisted them around. I have had doubt, fear, uncertainty, and a feeling of being lost. Did you know that God gave me a spirit of joy, peace, and sound mind? Your constant lies may have made me feel defeated and unworthy, but God made me victorious and knows the plans he has for me. His plans help me to prosper and not harm me; his plans give me a hope and a future. As for you, you want me destroyed and defeated. I have rebuked you numerous times and rebuked all you have tried to do to destroy my marriage, my children, and me. Well, your schemes and deceptions may come and go, but my God remains by my side, day and night. His word remains true and is engraved in my heart. I have hidden his word in my heart, so I will not sin against him. Don't you see, Satan? As for me and my house we will serve the Lord. We will serve the Lord, not you. I am a woman of faith, the daughter of the most high king. I can do all things with Christ, who strengthens me. I can cry out to my Jesus and know that it reaches his ears. The best part is—when I cry out to him—as long as I have the faith of a mustard seed, my prayers will be answered. And Satan, I will have the last laugh—the last laugh that will be filled with joy, knowing that God has, God will, and God forever shall be. You see, I am the wife of a police officer, the wife of a peacekeeper, and the wife of a son of God. I am the wife you need to worry about, because I know how powerful the name of Jesus is. I know how powerful the blood that was shed for me is. I will fight for my marriage, my family, and my life through the power of prayer and the powerful name of Jesus. So, Satan, beware of the wife who is a wife on duty. My duty is to serve my God, seek him all the days of my life, love the man God has placed in my life, and make certain that my home will be a home where God is at the center and is glorified.

Serving God with joy,
A wife on duty

The enemy should not be something we fear but something we look down at, because he has no authority. We should learn to laugh at his many failed attempts and praise God for the victories we have in situations that look like a failure. In laughing at the enemy, we will begin to see that walking by faith will become natural to us. Do not allow the enemy to have any access in your life; instead fill all areas with joy and thanksgiving.

REFLECTION

In all honesty, do you begin your day with prayer?

Have you ever considered praying about your husband's comings and goings while on duty?

What does the full armor of God mean to you? Do you feel as if you are geared up before you leave your house each day?

Write down the struggles you may be facing in your marriage. Look up Scriptures to stand on and speak that truth over the struggle you are facing. Document changes you see as you believe in God's truth over the situation.

Write down situations that you know irritate you and next to it write down a way that you can bring laughter or joy to the situation.

Write your own letter to Satan. Tell him the truth.

Father,

I praise you for each day and the many blessings and victories it holds. I ask that you equip me with the armor of God and help me recognize the tactics of the enemy. Give me wisdom to know how to pray for these situations and maintain a joyful spirit. I pray that your word will stay hidden in my heart so that I may not sin against you. I pray that while my husband is on duty, you will ordain his steps and protect him, both physically and spiritually. I pray that no weapon is formed against my family and that I will prosper. I pray that you will silence the deceiving tongue and that your word will be echoed in our hearts. We praise you for goodness and grace in our lives. We also praise you because you fight the battle for us and although we may grow weak and weary, we will renew our strength, and we will soar high like eagles. In you, my God, we will walk and not faint.

In Jesus' name,
Amen.

Chaplain Allison P. Uribe

TRUTH

_____,

(write your name above)

Put on the full armor of God, so that you can take your stand against the devil's schemes. For our struggle is not against flesh and blood, but against the rulers, against the authorities, against the powers of this dark world and against the spiritual forces of evil in the heavenly realms. Therefore put on the full armor of God, so that when the day of evil comes, you may be able to stand your ground, and after you have done everything, to stand (Ephesians 6: 11-13).

For his anger lasts only a moment, but his favor lasts a lifetime; weeping may stay for the night, but rejoicing comes in the morning (Psalm 30:5).

Your heavenly Father

CHAPTER 8

Triumph in His Name

"But thanks be to God, who always leads us in triumphal procession in Christ and through us spreads everywhere the fragrance of the knowledge of him" (2 Corinthians 2:14). As I learned to laugh at the enemy and his many attempts to attack my life and my marriage, I continued walking triumphantly. It is a promise I hold dear to my heart after my many years of hardship in my marriage, being a mother, and leading a ministry. Looking back, I see that all impossible situations become possible, and all the ashes become beautiful.

I did not know immediately that I had triumph; it was something I learned that God had given me as his daughter. I came into my marriage knowing of God but not walking with him. As I grew deeper in my walk with the Lord, I quickly learned that my heavenly Father wanted me, his daughter, to have the desires of my heart. I know this to be true, but as with anything, sometimes the desires we hold may not always be the wisest for our lives. I recall the numerous prayers I said when I was in my early twenties. I prayed for God to send me a husband because I longed to marry at a young age. Although I may have had a few heartbreaks, God knew exactly who I was destined to be with. He knew that my husband was to be my lifelong sweetheart. Had God answered me immediately, and I had married the first guy who came along, I wouldn't be living in such blessing. I was engaged to be married before I married my husband, but my ex-fiance called off the wedding. It was a blessing in disguise. I am not saying that my ex-fiance is not worthy or is an awful person, but God's plans allowed each of us to prosper. God had plans for him, and he had plans for me; they were not our own. God knows who we are to be with, and when we wait on him, his plans will give us a hope and a future. In that case, the plans he had for both my ex-fiance and me prospered in our future, and he placed us each with a spouse whom God knew would be suitable.

There are many times in our marriage when we pray for things that really will not allow us to prosper or benefit us in any way. I praise God that he knows my future, and because he holds my life in his hands, I know I have protection from harm. How often do we pray for our husband to change shifts or to move substations, only to see it not follow through? We must remember that we prayed and we presented our request to the Lord. Therefore, as believers, we must trust that God knows what is best for our family and our marriage. God hears our prayers and has ordained our time, our life, and all that is involved in it. We should trust that he knows and has his better plan at his perfect time.

In order to live in triumph, we also must remember the Ten Commandments. These commandments, given by God, do not make him a cruel, strict God but a loving God who shares all the things that can harm us and damage us, if we give in to them. He has given us these precious commandments as a shield from pain. I tell my children that we have rules not because we are mean parents but to protect them from getting hurt. God wants us to live in his triumph. It is up to us if we want to live according to his will and to follow these guidelines to protect ourselves. This also will keep our minds free of guilt and enable us to live in peace and with rest.

There are other areas in which we can choose to live triumphantly regardless of circumstances. When faced with a challenge, we either can choose to act or react. I would like to think that I would act in faith instead of reacting like a mad-woman. We may find ourselves in a number of situations that offer us an either/or choice. I will share a few of my life struggles in which I reacted, as well as those in which I acted.

In one particular situation, I found myself reacting. At the time, I thought my actions were relevant because the situation involved my son. Two years ago, our oldest son was diagnosed with celiac disease and this was something that hit our household hard. Celiac disease is a condition that damages the lining of the small intestine and causes the body to react adversely to gluten, which is found in wheat, barley, and rye. If not treated properly, celiac may lead to growth problems, siezures, or even intestinal cancer. Of course, the initial diagnosis brought us to tears, and we reacted immediately. We found ourselves struggling to find gluten-free food for a seven year-old, but we had no knowledge where to find it. It was such a feeling of loss and uncertainty, but that led me to cling to my faith even more. Of course, I questioned why and how my son had contracted this disorder, but those questions did not get me anywhere. I had to believe in my heart that God was still at work in my son's future and at work for us, as parents. As we learned more about the gluten sensitivity and where to find gluten-free aisles at the local grocery stores, our situation lightened up. I came to see that I had taken so much for granted, because I saw gluten-free cookies and pancake mix, and I cried at the store when I saw things that my child could eat. It was food that any seven year-old would love, and it brought me pure joy to see my son eating and truly enjoying his meal. I began to praise God for these findings at the grocery store. It is important to take joy in the little things so we can have joy in the bigger. We continue to believe in God to heal our son and know that God is truly at work, because our son was diagnosed with a disease that can be controlled. We praise God that our son is not dying and that all we have to do is alter his diet. I see that alone as a triumph. So I initially reacted, and then I acted.

In this next scenario, I acted and then reacted. In my marriage, there were times when I complained about my husband's sitting in front of the television or computer. I didn't appreciate it because as a housewife, I had no one to talk to all day, but when he got home, he didn't want to have long conversations. He wanted to sit back and relax in front of the television. I felt like I had no help and began to feel alone. I did my best not to let it consume me; I tried to look at the situation as a "WWJD" ("What would Jesus do?"). I acted but did not immediately react. As I kept on with my faith, I turned those agitations into a positive and looked for ways to be grateful. It was a challenge for me, but I enjoyed it, because I found it fun to seek positive in anything. When he was in front of the television for long periods, I would be grateful that he was home, instead of out with the guys, that he enjoyed being home, and that he was supporting us financially. Of course, I did pray for him and for God's will to be done in the way he spent his time. My staying positive and praying led to the victory we have now. My husband has thrown out our cable boxes, and television is a thing of the past in our home. My husband now says that he does not want anything to rob him of any time he has with his family. This took a few years of staying positive and remaining in prayer, but of course, triumph followed. God showed his faithfulness in that particular circumstance. My reactions were of praise then, and I do my best to see it remains like that in all that I face. Even though I try, however, I have to admit that I do have moments where I react.

Our marriage is a success today because of God and his holy works in our lives. As we go about our days, we forget to praise God for the simple and little things we enjoy. We forget to praise God for the many pairs of shoes we have, when there is someone out there with one pair. To see our life as plain is to deceive ourselves. On our morning drives, I love stopping at a traffic light so I can look out the window and admire the beauty of the sun and its brightness. When I see the sun in the morning, I look at it as God's saying "Good morning. I love you. I will light your day so you will not stumble. I see you and this day is for you. This day holds a blessing and triumph." We may face circumstances in our marriages that seem overwhelming and more dramatic than a husband sitting in front of the television, but God sees it all. Our tears and cries do not go unnoticed or unheard; they are acknowledged and made triumphant. It is up to us as to whether we will act in faith or react out of fear.

REFLECTION

What do you recognize as triumphs in your marriage?

Do you see yourself as a positive person? If not, why do you think you are not positive?

How will knowing you have triumph in Christ affect the way you see struggle or hardship?

In any situation you face, do you see yourself acting or reacting?

How can you change the way you see any challenges of the day?

Begin to have an attitude of gratitude. Make a list of things for which you are grateful.

Father,

Thank you for leading us into victory as wives and as your children. Help me act on faith and not react out of fear or discouragement. I pray that I will praise you in all things and see that you are working in my future so that I may have hope. I pray that you will help me to stay positive and show me the way I should go. I ask that my home will be full of joy and that my children and my children's children will live triumphant lives in you. I claim in your precious name that no matter how my marriage may be right now, it was destined to be triumphant and abounding in your grace. I ask that you give me wisdom on how to pray over my circumstances. I pray that doors will open that need to be and closed where I should not go. I ask that you will place me where you need me, and I trust that all my steps will be ordained by you.

In Jesus' name
Amen.

Chaplain Allison P. Uribe

TRUTH

_____,
(write your name above)

But thanks be to God! He gives us the victory through our Lord Jesus Christ (1 Corinthians 15:57).

For everyone born of God overcomes the world. This is the victory that has overcome the world, even our faith. (1 John 5:4).

Wealth and honor come from you; you are the ruler of all things. In your hands are strength and power to exalt and give strength to all. Now, our God, we give you thanks, and praise your glorious name (1 Chronicles 29: 12-13).

Your heavenly Father

CHAPTER 9

As for Me and My House

Once we are married, express our love, and recognize that our call as a wife is a good thing and that we have triumph with the God we serve, that brings us to our first ministry. Our first ministry begins in our home—what I like to call our heavenly substation. Our husbands have a hard time transitioning from uniformed officers to their family roles; they seem to let go slowly of their duty but not fully. It is like they go from one substation to another. As law enforcement wives, we may run our households in a unique way. For example, my home has cameras at every corner and three locks on the front door. Our side gates are bolted shut, and best of all, there is a security system. If you do not find that humorous, maybe this will make you laugh: A wife once told me that her husband would respond with "affirmative" when he agreed with something. These things are the sweetest part of being a law enforcement wife; we should view these little antics as a joy.

My household was guarded like Fort Knox and protected physically, but I was not sure if I was doing all I needed to protect it spiritually. We must make it a point to pray over our home at all times. I like to pray over my kitchen, that it will always have an abundance of food, that it will be filled with laughter, and full of many great conversations during meal-time, and that I will be able to bless others in my kitchen. There are many rooms

Chaplain Allison P. Uribe

and many requests we can pray for in our homes. I notice that when I do this, God really sees to it that my home remains in order. Proverbs 31:27 says, "She carefully watches everything in her household." We must keep a watchful eye as to how we run our household, whether we stay at home or work full time. Being watchful goes beyond knowing all the activity in your home; it is seeing to it that the setting or mood is a peaceful one. Our husbands' line of work has much chaos in it, so why would they want to go from chaos to chaos? We are human and will have days of discouragement and frustration, but the outcome of your day will all depend on how you handle those days. This is why God is such an important part of our daily lives. Growing accustomed to living in his word and focusing on the victory we have in him will almost diminish our once-great issues. It takes practice and dedication to see that our homes are in order and maintained in a peaceful manner. Our children should hold respect for both their father and mother. It is one of our commandments, and we as wives should see to it that they respect their father as head of the household. This can be done in a variety of ways, from being cautious in how we speak of our spouse in front of the children to keeping things from our spouse with regard to anything our children may have done wrong. Our children watch our every move and are said to do as they see at home. This is not always true, but if you have a toddler who speaks in defiance, and you wonder where those words came from, pay attention to your speech. Most times, those words are from your very mouth—I know that from experience. There was a time when I was busy with many projects, and my home was a mess. I was tired one day and that feeling of self-pity came over me. I remember blowing my hair out of my face and letting out a big sigh. I muttered, "I always have to do everything." These words would come back to haunt me later. Our youngest child is a little girl, and when I have asked her to clean her room, she throws her arms down, frowns, and says, "I always have to do everything." It makes me laugh now to wonder at how pitiful I must have looked that day in the kitchen, looking at the dishes in the sink and the many things on the counters. When she said those words, I told her that was not true and that it did not sound sweet coming out her mouth. I had to go back to the way I think God sees me when I make those comments. He is so graceful toward us that I cannot imagine his laughter as he watches us have our daily tantrums. This all goes back to being sure that our children show respect in our home, so it may carry on even outside of the home. We must show respect for what God asked us to do in Scripture. Of course, as we do this, we must do it all with grace.

We should step back and look at all the things that are a part of our household. It is important to see if the household is one of chaos or one of order. Once we set ourselves to a Christ-like mentality, we can further ourselves to an orderly life, where we hold wisdom and maintain self-control. Although we can do our best to see that order is in our home, we also should be aware that there will be many distractions. As the wife of an officer, we find ourselves busy and occupied in every area of our life. We have many demands to meet each day and roles to play. But I ask you this: what keeps you from being the wife or mother your household needs?

For example, I am on the computer quite often, tending to ministry business and emails and with my studies. My husband came into the room one day and said, "Oh, you're on the computer." Now, these words may sound harmless, but it was the sarcasm in his voice that got my immediate attention.

I stopped what I was doing and went to him to ask if he was all right. He said, "Yeah, why?" I responded, "Well, you don't seem too happy that I am on the computer. I am just doing some ministry work. I will be off in a minute. Are you sure you don't need anything?" He then said," It's not that, but honey, you always seem to be doing something on the computer and even more so on my days off." I said, "Well honey, I am just doing ministry things. I didn't know you felt that way. I'm sorry. I can get off." He just carried on with what he was doing and after that, I got off the computer—and then my mind began to wonder about what he said. Were there things or distractions in my life that kept me from seeing the ways of my household? I go about my daily routine—I cook, clean, kiss and hug my husband when he returns home, tend to the children, and attend to my chaplain duties, and God gives me the grace and time to do it. What more could I do? This was something I had to pray about and asked God for wisdom. After thinking about my husband's comment that day and noticing the looks he would give me when I was on the computer, I thought I would discuss this with him. Our discussion was a success, and I admitted that there were a lot of distractions in my life that would make my husband or children feel robbed of time with me. These distractions ranged from taking phone calls at wrong times, getting on social networks or the computer (whether it be for ministry or pleasure), and attending too many events that required me to be away from my home. So how do I manage all this? God answered me. He always hears our prayers, and he answers. First, I will serve my God. Serving my God will help me to be a great helper to my husband and keeper of my home. With the peace and joy of the Lord and his word as a lamp to my feet, I will be able to be a great servant of God. When I put those two together—a keeper of my home and a helper to my spouse—I also am serving my God. How? Because God called me to be helper!

My husband was not happy with the amount of time I spent on the computer. I could have easily become upset and could have told him that he would just have to deal with it, or I could have just ignored his reactions to my time on the computer. Of course, my husband is someone I respect, honor, and love. I vowed to love him for better or worse—I vowed before God. So naturally, I care about his feelings and concerns. No matter what comes our way in life, we must remember that our home is our first ministry. Is it yours? Sometimes Satan can use your good intentions and your big heart to keep you from being a keeper of your home. Going back to Proverbs 31:27, I love that it says "she carefully watches." Did you catch that? "She carefully watches." When we allow too many distractions we will not be able to watch over what God has assigned us first. We all have many responsibilities and different roles, but when the Lord ordains each of them, God will see to it that you have time to manage all. So I ask you, what items are on your plate that don't fit? What do you notice as distractions in your life? What keeps you so busy that it takes away from quality time with your spouse, your children, and your home?

"Who can find a virtuous and capable wife? She is worth more than precious rubies. Her husband can trust her, and she will greatly enrich his life. She will not hinder him but help him all her life" (Proverbs 31:10-12). Wives on duty, what are you doing? What are you sacrificing in your life to enrich the lives of your precious family or to enrich the life of your husband? As wives of officers, we must use wisdom and ask our heavenly Father for it often. Our homes should be filled with grace and joy. As a wife on duty, let's declare Joshua 24:15—"But as for me and my household, we will serve the Lord."

If we have a home that is God-centered, we will have a home that is heavenly and in it, we will find an outstanding marriage that will magnify our blessings, and our family will be exceptional.

H – Heavenly
O – Outstanding
M – Magnificent
E – Exceptional

REFLECTION

Are there distractions that keep you from being the wife or mother your household needs?

Draw a picture of a plate, and then write out all your obligations on it, and see how full your plate is. Then pray about what needs to be removed.

What do you notice are distractions in your life?

What keeps you so busy that it takes away quality time with your spouse, your children, and your home?

Do you have a hard time saying "no" to others?

Father,

I thank you for the household and family you have blessed me with. I come to you seeking wisdom and how better to watch the things of my household. Help me recognize anything that may harm my children or my marriage. As I live my life, help me to manage my time and make it pleasing to you. I ask that you reveal anything that is distracting me daily or keeping me from being able to spend time reading your word or simply just being in your presence. Help me to know that I can say no to others in a healthy way and set my priorities so that others will know of my responsibilities. I thank you, Lord, for helping me as I journey through this life and for watching over my household when I can't. I pray that our home will be Christ-centered and that my husband will seek you and lead our family into your grace and love. I pray that even with the busyness of life, our home will be a home of order. I pray that my home will be heavenly and my marriage would be outstanding, that we will reap magnificent blessings, and that our home will be exceptional because you dwell there. Help me to be a wife on duty who builds up my home. Thank you, Lord, for all the glorious things you have done and will continue to do in our home.

In Jesus' name,
Amen.

TRUTH

_____,

(write your name above)

Wives, in the same way submit yourselves to your own husbands so that, if any of them do not believe the word, they may be won over without words by the behavior of their wives (1 Peter 3:1).

The wise woman builds her house, but with her own hands the foolish one tears hers down (Proverbs 14:1).

Charm is deceptive, and beauty is fleeting; but a woman who fears the Lord is to be praised (Proverbs 31:30).

Let us not become weary in doing good, for at the proper time we will reap a harvest if we do not give up. Therefore, as we have opportunity, let us do good to all people, especially to those who belong to the family of believers (Galatians 6:9-11).

Your heavenly Father

CHAPTER 10

The Pursuit

In the line of duty, officers will end up in a pursuit at times. These pursuits are a chase to capture those who have violated the law. However, the pursuit I speak of is seeking to have an unshakeable faith and just like a pursuit, daring to go into the unknown. As I have said, it is all about keeping our focus on God. When I think of the pursuit in my life to follow God and seek his will, I read about Peter on the boat. This is found in Matthew 14:22-33.

Immediately Jesus made the disciples get into the boat and go on ahead of him to the other side, while he dismissed the crowd. After he had dismissed them, he went up on a mountainside by himself to pray. Later that night, he was there alone, and the boat was already a considerable distance from land, buffeted by the waves because the wind was against it. Shortly before dawn, Jesus went out to them, walking on the lake. When the disciples saw him walking on the lake, they were terrified. "It's a ghost," they said, and cried out in fear. But Jesus immediately said to them: "Take courage! It is I. Don't be afraid."

"Lord, if it's you," Peter replied, "tell me to come to you on the water." "Come," he said. Then Peter got down out of the boat, walked on the water and came toward Jesus. But when he saw the wind, he was afraid and, beginning to sink, cried out, "Lord, save me!" Immediately Jesus reached out his hand and caught him. "You of little faith," he said, "why did you doubt?" And when they climbed into the boat, the wind died down. Then those who were in the boat worshiped him, saying, "Truly you are the Son of God."

How often we do we have our Peter moments? These are moments where we find ourselves bold in the Lord, ready to take on his tasks, and daring to believe the impossible. Then, the winds of life blow around us, and we take notice of it. The wind that blows around us are like the distractions the enemy tries to bring so that we will take our focus off God and begin to have doubt and fear. Just like Peter, at times we dare to step out of the boat and once something doesn't look right, we cry for help and react in panic. The earth is the Lord's, and it is full of his glory and creations. The wind is a creation of the Lord. As I read this, I remember that our God promises to give us beauty for our ashes. This means that whatever the enemy uses to try to harm us, God turns it around in our favor. This is expressed when Peter cries out to God. I love that although he stepped out of boat in boldness and came to have fear or doubt, he knew that the son of man would immediately lift him up. Even before Peter stepped out of the boat, Jesus already had told him to "come." His words were not to come and be cautious but to come and follow. This is why we should walk by faith and not by sight.

Peter moments can sharpen us as we pursue an unshakeable faith. "You open your hand and satisfy the desires of every living thing. The Lord is righteous in all his ways and faithful in all he does (Psalm 145:16-17). We must remember that we can use each day and each circumstance we face to benefit our future. James 1:2-4 says, "Consider it pure joy, my brothers and sisters, whenever you face trials of many kinds, because you know that the testing of your faith produces perseverance. Let perseverance finish its work so that you may be mature and complete, not lacking anything."

Only God can turn our worst life circumstances into something so great that all we can do is rise. This is why testimonies can be so effective, and we should pursue being real women of God. He makes all things new, and we must choose to move forward. Just be a vessel, and let God do the rest, with your faith fully in the Lord. We must walk by faith and not by sight, because it is not you but God in you who can do all things.

Going back to Peter, I noticed that he cried for help, knowing that the others would hear him. He was not ashamed to admit that he had fear and was frightened of sinking into the ocean. Before he stepped out of the boat, I can only imagine his boldness. He was a disciple of Christ, and like many of us, dared to be so bold. There are times in life when even we as Christian women can use our boldness as arrogance. As we pursue being more godly and seek God's will, let us not forget that we will fall short of his glory all the days of our lives. No matter how much we pursue God, we should never consider ourselves above anyone. We should not be ashamed of our trials and tribulations but instead embrace them, so that when the time comes we can speak of the many glorious things that God pulled us out of.

In the beginning years of Wives on Duty Ministries, I struggled with that very concept. I shared my many struggles in reverence to those who I knew would be blessed by it. But as years went on and the ministry grew, sharing my trials and tribulations was no longer acceptable to me. My church had asked me if I would be a part of their chaplaincy team. When I became a chaplain, that title changed everyone's view of me and the way I live. I say "that title," because although I am proud of it, it is just a title. The title holds no power; only God holds power. Many women saw me as a godly woman who was above all struggles. They felt my walk was deeper than anyone else's because of my title. It really hurt me to hear them say, "I don't know how you do it, but you always have it together." They were right that I maintained self-control about my life, but it was the fact that they saw me as woman without struggle that bothered me. Of course, that is impossible, because no matter how deep we get in our walk with the Lord, our struggles are what make us who we are today. Our struggles will be the testimonies that may save another person's life from defeat and doubt.

I went through a time of feeling fake about my walk with God. I went from feeling discouraged about letting others down and not being an example of hope, to wanting to share my struggles so that I could express hope. God showed me that in sharing my struggles, so many would find hope. Although my journey began years ago, I am still walking with my Lord and he is still the Lord of my life and helps me through all my weaknesses.

Like many other law enforcement wives, I go through my own marital struggles. I have the same mood swings as everyone else and get discouraged at times. I have heard from many wives that they feel as if they have to maintain constant joy, because their husbands sometimes have sudden outbursts of anger. Our spouses, at times, cannot separate their authoritative tone on duty to the authoritative tone with their children or their wives. Many wives feel as if their spouses treat them like a subject they deal with on the streets. Have you ever felt that you snap at your children for such small things and hope that when your spouse is there, he will make up for your snaps and be gentle-spirited with them? Of course, when this doesn't happen, it just brings you right back down into the pit of discouragement and defeat.

There are also times when law enforcement wives have a spouse who is away from home so much that they begin to feel like single parents. They are the ones who dress the children, feed them, get them onto their daily activities, and lay them down at night, all without their husbands' physical help. There also could be the circumstances in which you are at the dinner table, and his pager or cell phone goes off because there is a homicide or an investigation that needs to be started.

One struggle with which we all can relate as law enforcement families is having to face the many prejudices the community holds toward the police departments. My middle child came home from school one day and told me that a little girl in his class said that all police officers are bad. This made my son sad, because she was essentially saying that his daddy was bad. My son looks up to his father, and he wants to be an officer when he grows up. I hugged him and apologized that he had to hear that. I then told him we needed to pray for this family, and if he was upset with the little girl, he needed to forgive her. There will always be prejudice in this world but expressing anger toward it will do us no good. Even God says, "starting a quarrel is like breaching a dam; so drop the matter before a dispute breaks out" (Proverbs 17:14) Two wrongs do not make a right. That is why it is important to focus on God and do as he has asked of us in this life. I tell you this not to shine a light on struggles but for you to know that you are not alone in your pursuit to fight for your marriages and your homes. We must use these against the tactics that the enemy presents to us to obtain our victory. We fight through these battles as wives on duty so that we may be walking testimonies of God's holy works. The most precious promise to me—and each time I say it in faith, it brings me to tears—is found in Isaiah 40:28-31.

Do you not know? Have you not heard?

The Lord is the everlasting God, the Creator of the ends
of the earth.

He will not grow tired or weary, and his understanding
no one can fathom.

He gives strength to the weary and increases the power
of the weak.

Even youths grow tired and weary, and young men
stumble and fall; but those who hope in the Lord
will renew their strength.

They will soar on wings like eagles; they will run and
not grow weary,

They will walk and not be faint.

This specific passage is my prayer for the wives of law enforcement, firemen, and all emergency personnel. We face unique challenges in our marriage that probably no other marriages face, but the one thing that is the same is the promise our days hold in God. As we pursue growing deeper in the Lord and fighting for our marriages, remember that these struggles are nothing to be ashamed of. All human beings in the world face struggles. The only shame there might be in the struggles is what we choose to do with them. What do I mean? As women in Christ and as sisters in the law enforcement family, we must have respect, love, and compassion enough to hold others' struggles with much care. The sad truth is that many departments are faced with gossip, and that can diminish anybody's trust in seeking help. When you reach out to others or others reach out to you, respect God's children and see to it that when they seek encouragement, you do not look down on them. Instead, look them in the eye, believe there will be a miracle, and lift them up in prayer.

God and Wives on Duty Ministries is now my life pursuit. Our mission statement is to support and encourage wives through the word of God. It's time to stand up and not allow our marriages to be stolen; it's time to seek to live an extraordinary life. Let's rise above our pride and help each other in this life we walk through. Putting the blame on others and their actions makes us no different from the rest. Seek to find a prayer partner you can trust or someone who will be encouraging and not discouraging. Pursue the vision that God has for your life and marriage. Remember to stay focused on the one who loved you first—God.

REFLECTION

Read Matthew 14:22-33. What life circumstances do you find yourself in that keep you from getting out of the boat and into the walk of faith?

Have you had Peter moments, where you were bold in your faith but something happened to shake your faith a bit?

Take the struggles you are facing now and write out ways that you will show your "stepping out of the boat" boldness.

Do you find you are a woman who looks down on others and judges their weaknesses?

Our law enforcement family is hurting nationally, either through marital struggles, divorce, or suicide, or even with the act of gossip in the departments. How will you choose to act when others seek your help or if you hear of another's struggles?

Do you find yourself surrounded by those who speak poorly of others? Will you continue to allow this or take part in such conversations?

Father,

I want to pursue more of you. I pray that as I seek you more, I will recognize that my daily struggles will not only sharpen me but allow me to be a blessing by giving hope to others. Help me to remember my struggles are just victories. I praise you that you will give me beauty for ashes. I pray for the many wives out there, like me, who are hurting. I pray that if someone seeks encouragement that I will uphold all she shares with respect and leave it in your hands. Help me to stand up at this time and join the victorious battle we face in our departments. Help me to see myself and others as a human being and nothing greater.

In Jesus' name,
Amen.

Chaplain Allison P. Uribe

TRUTH

_____,

(write your name above)

If anyone speaks, they should do so as one who speaks the very words of God. If anyone serves, they should do so with the strength God provides, so that in all things God may be praised through Jesus Christ. To him be the glory and the power for ever and ever (1 Peter 4:11).

So do not fear, for I am with you; do not be dismayed, for I am your God. I will strengthen you and help you; I will uphold you with my righteous right hand. (Isaiah 41:10)

But the Lord stood at my side and gave me strength, so that through me the message might be fully proclaimed and all the Gentiles might hear it. And I was delivered from the lion's mouth (2 Timothy 4:17).

Your heavenly Father

CHAPTER 11

And They Lived Happily Ever After

As a wife of an officer, I find my job—my duty—to be an honorable one. My journey is ongoing, and I look forward to the rest of it. Looking back to the moment I walked down the aisle, I am in awe of the many testimonies God has placed in my life. When I got married, I had no idea of the strength I would have, once Christ became a part of my marriage. I had no idea just how suitable God saw me as my husband's wife. It was a transformation of my heart, and it still is being transformed today. I love seeing the many challenges my marriage faced years ago as a testimony now. I gained more knowledge and learned each step of the way with the Lord as my guide.

Having God in your life does not mean you will not have trials and that you live happily ever after, but it does mean that when you have trials, you will know the battle is won, and you can live happily ever after. Living with joy brings about a transformation of the heart. A few years back, our middle son, who was five years old at the time, told me he wanted to give his heart to Jesus. He said he wanted to be good, which meant changing his behavior. Of course, I was thrilled and prayed with my son, knowing that the enemy would not be happy about this. That dedication of his life brought about many challenges for him. We noticed his behavior was odd, and he was doing things out of the norm. We had stayed in prayer over him and continued to pray protection as he began his walk with the Lord. One night, as he lay down to go to bed, he looked sad, and I asked him what was wrong. He said, "Mama, I am so bad, and I sin so much that I think Jesus is going to give my heart back to me." Of course it hurt me to hear this, and I began to cry. I told him that I knew how hard it was to try and not mess up. I told him how precious and good he was. I told him how, most important, he was to remember why Jesus died on the cross. "Jesus died for you because he knew you would not be perfect. He knew you were going to lie to Mommy today. He knew you were going to hit your brother and fight with your sister. He knew you were not going to listen when I asked you to do something today. Jesus died for you so your heart could stay with Jesus forever, and you and he could be together forever. Jesus was so happy when you gave him your heart that he wants to hold onto it until the day you see him again." While I was telling my son just how worthy of God's grace he was and how precious he was, I cried more, because I know that God loves my son so much more than I ever could.

A few days passed, and as my son ran off to play, I called to him. He turned around, and I told him that one of the things I love about him is that he has a giving heart and shares very well. He smiled and said, "I do that because God gave me a new heart and loves me." I could see the joy in his little face as he told me that. He had an assurance, knowing he was a child of God. Wives on duty, you are daughters of a king! Know your worth! In many fairy tales, the princess is deceived by a wicked being, but in the end, she is rescued. Our lives are such a tale of triumph. Our King, our Prince Charming husbands, and us, as the daughters of a King, continue to seek our happily ever after with a God who makes all things possible and gives us unimaginable strength. So pursue first the kingdom of God, and you, too, will have your happily-ever-after marriage. Remember how precious you are and how worthy you are to receive God's infinite grace and unconditional love. You may mess up, time and time again, but your heart is what God sees. He knows when you are trying and when you are sorry. But above all, he has ordained you as a suitable helper. Ask God to help you with your weaknesses in this life and on this journey. It will allow him to turn those weaknesses into strengths. Allow him to take your hurt, pain, transgressions, and sorrow, and turn it into an awesome testimony. A friend once told me that when she goes running she looks down at her feet. She looks down because she feels that if she looks ahead, she may get tired easily, distracted by the long, hard distance, and might stop running before she reaches her goal. How many of us are running and focusing on the difficulties or obstacles we see? How many of us are so close to our happily ever after? "Now faith is being sure of what we hope for and certain of what we do not see" (Hebrews11:1). It's time to focus on the task at hand. The word declares that one can chase a thousand, and two can put ten thousand to flight. It's time to rise and lift one another, with God as our backup. We should be living examples of for better or worse. In our greatest praise, it is then that all things bound in our lives will be loosed. We must not give place to the enemy with our words, negative emotions, or lack of forgiveness. Instead, we must hold on to the promises that we have been given to hold each day we live. God will confirm his word in our life when we forgive, praise, seek him, and have faith. Maintain a joy in your life because he has overcome and the impossible will be possible. Let us now gather as wives on duty and put ten thousand to flight. God loves you so much more than anyone on this earth ever could. He does love you as he loved his son, Jesus. He knows your days that lie ahead and what they hold. As I continue to journey through this life, my story continues. The creator of the heavens and the earth had prewritten my days, and each day holds so many promises and new beginnings. I live each day, ready to learn and gain more wisdom. I may never get to the point of full understanding in this life, but for now and always, I will live to serve my God who has continued to give me victory. At the end of each day, I hope that I did my best for the Lord, and he has a smile on his face. Take this journey and embrace it. From one wife on duty to another, be sure to find peace and joy in the Father.

REFLECTION

"For the revelation awaits an appointed time; it speaks of the end and will not prove false. Though it linger, wait for it; it will certainly come and will not delay" (Habakkuk 2:3). Now that you have read this Scripture, write down the desires of your heart for your marriage.

After you have written the desires of your heart for your marriage, title it, "My Journey as a Wife on Duty". Begin to pray about the things you seek for your marriage and be sure to document all God does.

Live in your happily ever-after with God at the center of your marriage. What will this mean for your marriage?

Father,

Thank you for this calling on my life as the wife of a law enforcement officer. I want to be more like you each day and seek first your kingdom and all righteousness. I praise you for the victory I have in you. I will leave my requests with you in regards to my marriage, children, work, and finances. I pray that you heal my heart from any hidden pain. Thank you Lord for making all things new and bringing me to a path of happiness and joy. I pray that my life will be a living example of your love. I praise you for your great works and never-failing love in my life. You are my everlasting God who brings healing and restoration.

In Jesus' name,
Amen.

TRUTH

_____,

(write your name above)

For everything that was written in the past was written to teach us, so that through the endurance taught in the Scriptures and the encouragement they provide we might have hope (Romans 15:4).

"What no eye has seen, what no ear has heard, and what no human mind has conceived the things God has prepared for those who love him (1 Corinthians 2:9).

Be strong and courageous. Do not be afraid or terrified because of them, for the Lord your God goes with you; he will never leave you nor forsake you" (Deuteronomy 31:6).

Your heavenly Father

Wives on Duty,

Be confident of this, that he who began a good work in you will carry it on to completion until the day of Christ Jesus (Philippians 1:6).

To God be the glory!
Not the end, but the beginning

Prayers of A Wife On Duty

DEDICATED TO THE HEROES BEHIND THE HEROES
"Pray without ceasing" (1 Thessalonians 5:17)

First and foremost I pray for the safety of my husband and his co-workers. Another *huge* request is for my husband to find comfort in God's love. I want God as the center of my marriage. I know he loves God, but having not grown up in a very religious/ spiritual household he finds prayer and praise.—Police wife

I pray with my son the same prayer, before or as my husband goes to work. We pray, "Dear Lord, please watch over my daddy. We ask that you protect his heart, his mind, his body, and his soul from all evil. We pray you can use him to reach someone in need and then bring him home safely to us. In your Son's name, amen."—Police wife

"Father, protector of all that is righteous and good, please continue to keep him safe from all of the evil that surrounds him. Protect him, bring him home safe, and give him the peace of your presence in the midst of utter chaos. Above all, guard his heart from all that the enemy tries to pierce it with. Keep his eyes and heart always on you, Lord, and may he pursue you with a love that is deeper than even his love for me. Give him a heart to share your love with others who so desperately need it, which I know is well beyond his comfort zone. God, I pray he realizes your true potential in him and the call you have on his life. I pray the same courage to pursue a spiritually lost brother in blue as he has to pursue an armed criminal in a high-speed chase. Bring peace to the city he serves that is so broken and desperate. I know all of this is only possibly through you, God, and I am eternally grateful for all you continue to give to us and do for us."—Police wife

I think the one prayer that plays out several times a day is "Lord, please keep him safe and bring him back home to me!" I also pray that he can stay strong in his faith when he is constantly bombarded by evil.—Police wife

My prayer includes not only his physical safety, but all the emotional safety of our marriage. The never-ending exposure to the darkness that society has to offer and the consumption of his time and patience can place incredible strain on relationships, communication, and commitments. At times, as a wife of an officer it can feel overwhelming and lonely. I pray that in times when this divide feels deep and wide, that we will find one another on the other side as one.—Police wife

St. Michael the archangel, defend us in battle; be our protection against the malice and snares of the devil. May God rebuke him, we humbly pray; and thou, oh Prince of the heavenly host, by the power of God, thrust into hell Satan and all evil spirits who wander through the world for the ruin of souls. Amen—Police wife

I am always in prayer that God will cross my husband's path with someone who has been positively impacted by law enforcement. I know it is so important for him to see the good that his job does, even if it is not him directly. I pray that a thank-you is uttered in the moments when his heart is feeling hardened and that angels help him keep heavenly perspective.—Police wife

I pray that he comes home safely after every shift. I also pray for those who have brought harm, stress and discontent to our home.—Police wife

Father, I ask that you protect my husband in every way each day. I pray that he will be a blessing to so many and that you will use him as your vessel as he protects and serves our city. I ask that you will bring him home safely to us. Please protect his heart from all he will see. Give him a spirit of peace as he deals with aggressive people. I pray that above all, your will be done in his life.—Police wife

God, please restore my marriage and keep our home protected. I pray against divorce and that you will give me strength as a wife. Help me to forgive my husband for hurting me in the past and allow me to forward in your name. Amen—Military wife

Protect my husband each day. Keep him safe and under your watch. Help me not to be fearful of all his job requires. Give me a peace of mind while he works.—Fire Dept. wife

Our marriage is suffering right now and I am asking our Lord to intervene. I do not have the answers but know God put me as this officer's wife, and so he will see me through it. I want more closeness, trust, and for my husband to know I am his friend; not one of his subjects in the streets. I am to be trusted. You know my heart, Lord. Now please help us and help him. In Jesus' name I pray.—Police wife

Thank you to all the wives on duty who shared their prayer requests. May the Lord grant you the desires of your heart.

Wives On Duty Ministries

What is Wives on Duty? What does it mean to be a wife on duty? Wives on Duty is a faith-based ministry designed to encourage wives of law enforcement through the word of God. That's you! Wives on Duty believes in spreading the Gospel of Jesus Christ and encouraging wives of officers with the truth. You were called to be a helper to your spouse. "The Lord God said, It is not good for man to be alone. I will make a helper suitable for him." You are suitable! You are suitable to meet the needs of your husband's heart and to be the wife God has called you to be. God has blessed you with this amazing role as the wife of an officer. Being the wife of a law enforcement officer has so many unique challenges and yet so much beauty, that no other marriage other than your own could comprehend. I encourage you to read your Bible daily and as you go through it, seek God's wisdom and guidance as you journey through this life in this important role. Remember, the word of God says that you can do all things through Christ who strengthens you. Wives on Duty, it's time to seek first the kingdom of God. I pray that this book will be a blessing to you as I share my own journey and share the victories in my marriage to which only God himself has led me. To God be the glory!

www.wivesonduty.com

How can you start a Wives on Duty chapter in your area?

First, contact your local police chaplain to see if this is something she may want to oversee or pursue for the wives in your department. You also may ask a chaplain or minister in your church. The goal is to have all Wives on Duty leaders equipped in ministry. Once you have someone to take on leadership, have her contact Wives on Duty at wivesonduty@att.net and we will send a starter kit. Of course before pursuing this idea, be sure to pray that it is God's will for your department wives.

Current Wives On Duty Chapters

San Antonio, Texas
Chaplain Allison P. Uribe
wivesonduty@att.net

Modesto, California
Chaplain Lori Gomes
GomesL@modestopd.com

Johnson County, Texas
Chaplain Lisa Lerner
blessthebadge@att.net

About The Author

Allison P. Uribe is the wife of a San Antonio police officer. She and her husband have three beautiful children, two boys and a girl. She is a stay at-home mother and homeschools her children. Allison grew up in a military family and traveled from city to city and from the United States to Europe. She is the only daughter with an older brother who also joined the armed forces. Both her brother and father are retired from the US Air Force. She is the proud aunt to five nieces and nephew and one grandniece, making her parents the grandparents of nine. Her mother and father have been married for thirty-four years and have been a great example of what a marriage should be. Allison enjoys writing, watching movies, acting, playing basketball, and having breakfast tacos with close friends. She is a graduate of Providence High School and attended Our Lady of the Lake University in San Antonio, Texas. Currently, she is a lead community chaplain seeking to become ordained through the Assemblies of God. She has been a student in the Emergency Services Chaplains Program and now is a student at Global University Berean School of the Bible, in pursuit of her minister's license. She continues to pursue her education in ministry. Recently a big door opened for her with the San Antonio Police Department and she became a San Antonio police auxiliary chaplain. As the wife of an officer she has learned that her marriage is unique and in a class of its own. Her heart is now to reach out to wives of officers everywhere. As the founder and chaplain of Wives on Duty Ministries, Allison has a dream of traveling as a speaker and being able to encourage, hug, and love the wives of law enforcement officers, firefighters, and military nationwide.